Kids n't

I0360244

# KIDS who FOLLOW, KIDS who DON'T

Formerly *How to Really Know Your Child*

# ROSS CAMPBELL, M.D.
## WITH PAT LIKES

# VICTOR BOOKS®
### A DIVISION OF SCRIPTURE PRESS PUBLICATIONS INC.
### USA CANADA ENGLAND

*The stories told in this book are based on real case histories. However, names and details have been changed to prevent identification. If you think you see yourself or your neighbor herein, you are really seeing the problems and challenges faced by all parents.*

Unless otherwise indicated, Scripture quotations are from the *Holy Bible, New International Version*, © 1973, 1978, 1984, International Bible Society. Used by permission of Zondervan Bible Publishers. Also quoted is the *New American Standard Bible* (NASB), © the Lockman Foundation 1960, 1962, 1963, 1968, 1971, 1972, 1973, 1975, 1977.

*Second Printing, 1989*

Recommended Dewey Decimal Classification: 155.4-155.5

Suggested Subject Heading: CHILDREN—TRAINING

Library of Congress Catalog Card Number: 89-60181

ISBN: 0-89693-759-3

# CONTENTS

*To my children,*
CAREY, CATHY, DAVID, *and* DALE,
*who have been my best teachers.*

# Foreword

As I read the manuscript for this book for the very first time, I thought, "At last, a book that dispels both the ultraliberal and ultraconservative theories of Christian child-rearing."

We are bombarded today with so many different ideas on successful parenting that most parents are confused, and rightfully so. What we need is good, sound advice, not theory. We are looking for practical, usable Christian ethics and attitudes to help us bring the children in our care to responsible adulthood. How grateful I am to Dr. Ross Campbell for giving the public this very information.

I must confess that I was only lukewarm about reading this book in the beginning. My reaction was, "Oh, no, not another one!" My children are teenagers so I am fairly well read on the current books on raising teens and preteens, and I have had a lot of experience working with the young people of our church, so I didn't think I could learn anything new.

Nonetheless, I have been concerned about our young people, not just in our church, but throughout the nation. How are we failing them? Where are they going spiritually? What can we as parents and Christians do about it? How pleasantly surprised I was to find answers to all these questions in this book.

I am impressed by Dr. Campbell's sound advice, but more than anything, I am impressed by his deep concern for our young people. This book is not another cold and clinical text, but a warm and wise appeal for basic Christianity to begin at home.

Our families will only be truly stable when we make practical

Christianity the foundation for our lives. Dr. Campbell knows and tells us that unconditional, Christlike love is the beginning of that foundation.

*Kids Who Follow, Kids Who Don't* taught me many things. Not only did I gain insight into my own children, but I related to the problems of the parents interviewed.

Whether you are a parent or a grandparent, whether your child is two or twenty-two, this book is a must for you.

Mrs. *Connie Jenkins*
Wife of a United Methodist Pastor
Central Illinois Conference
(and mother of three teenagers)

# Preface

In January 1986, I met Dr. Ross Campbell of Signal Mountain, Tennessee, and during the ensuing weeks as his cowriter, I became the first parent to benefit from *Kids Who Follow, Kids Who Don't.* However, I am not the first to benefit from his wise and understanding counsel, for Dr. Campbell has spent many years as an internationally known child psychiatrist helping parents and children. And after working with him on this project, I know his work has been a labor of love.

Putting in writing his beliefs and experiences has taught me more about myself and my children than I thought possible. The most important lesson I learned was that in order for a child to develop as a Christian, he must first develop as a *whole* individual. As Dr. Campbell puts it, "Develop the *whole* child. Don't just zero in on the spiritual area of his life and expect everything else to fall into place—it won't."

Dr. Campbell obviously loves children. By patiently and clearly explaining their basic needs, he teaches *us* how to love *our* children. From experience, he knows that the first and most basic need in a child is the need for love—unconditional love.

In this book, Dr. Campbell shares two decades of knowledge in a simple, straightforward way. He gives you no pat answers; he has no tricks. Instead he offers good, commonsense advice. He never tells you child-rearing is easy; he only knows the challenge is of infinite worth.

I have met few people who care as deeply for the welfare of children as Dr. Ross Campbell. The phone in his car isn't tucked neatly into a little cubbyhole collecting dust; it is well used. I wondered, as he drove me to the airport after our last meeting, how many times he had started up Signal Mountain after a long and exhausting day, only to pick up that ringing phone and hear, "Dr. Campbell, you're needed at the hospital."

But I didn't wonder what he said to his caller because Ross Campbell loves children.

*Pat Likes*
Barry, Illinois

# 1

# Will Your Children Carry On Your Faith?

*"After that whole generation had been gathered up to their fathers, another generation grew up, who knew neither the Lord nor what He had done for Israel"* (Judges 2:10).

The smartly dressed middle-aged couple stepped nervously into my office.

I glanced at their names on my appointment schedule: John and Mary Perkins. The notation underneath said they had a fifteen-year-old, unmarried, pregnant daughter.

They took seats across from my desk. Mary, a stunning blond, looked familiar. "We've met somewhere. More than once, haven't we?" I asked.

She managed a tight smile. "I've shown you to a table several times at the Sailmaker Restaurant."

"You're the hostess there at lunch. I was there last Tuesday."

I turned to John and asked about his work. "I'm an accountant," he said.

"That figures," I punned, trying to lighten the air.

We spent another minute or two on small talk and found we had mutual friends at the Presbyterian church where they were members.

I glanced down at my appointment notes, then looked up at Mary. "You came in to talk about your daughter, Ann. Tell me about her."

Tears welled up in the mother's eyes. "Oh, Dr. Campbell, she's only fifteen. Just a year out of junior high. The youngest of our four. And she's pregnant! What are we going to do?"

The words were gushing now and she kept dabbing at her eyes. "We did everything we knew to be good parents to Ann. We've both worked for years to give her and our other children the good things in life. We took her to Sunday School and church. We gave her piano lessons and sent her to summer camp. She's so talented and beautiful. But how are we going to handle *this?*" Her voice trailed off in sobs as her husband twisted in his chair.

"I just don't know where we went wrong," John Perkins added. "Why did she get herself into this mess? Why has she become so defiant? She goes against anything and everything her mother and I try to do for her."

After spending about an hour with John and Mary, I realized that they really loved Ann, but communicated their feelings to her by giving her material things. They honestly felt that this would make up for not being able to spend time with her or share in her life.

Then I spoke with Ann. My suspicions were confirmed. Ann did not feel her parents loved her. She did not feel she was important to them.

"I don't know why I got pregnant; I just did. I could have kept from it. I knew how," Ann stated defiantly. "Maybe I wanted to be somebody too, like my mother. Maybe I thought if I was a mother, then I would be important—*somebody* would love *me.*"

For the next month, John, Mary, and Ann came for counseling on a weekly basis. At first, the sessions were reserved; few feelings were openly stated. Ann usually had little to say; she was obviously angry and frustrated. But after two or three weeks, she began to open up.

"Remember the night of the mother-daughter banquet,

## Will Your Children Carry On Your Faith?

Mom?" Ann asked. "You couldn't be there because you had to go with Daddy to that accountant's seminar or whatever it was. I was the only one there without a mother!"

"But, Ann," Mary interrupted, "we talked about it, and I bought you that lovely yellow dress for the banquet. I thought you didn't mind that I went with Daddy."

"Well, I did! You guys just never seem to be around when I need you. My friends' parents always drive us to games and stuff; you guys never offer to drive. I'm always bumming rides with someone. You guys never take me and my friends anywhere."

"Now wait a minute, Ann," her father retaliated. "You're talking like we never do anything for you. I happen to know that you're quite an accomplished pianist. Who took you to all those lessons? Who paid for all of them?"

"Big deal, Daddy. Anyway, how would you know whether or not I can play the piano? The last time you attended one of my recitals I was ten years old!"

During outbursts like these, John would often leave the room. But gradually both he and Mary began to understand their daughter's feelings. They realized that the *things* they had given Ann could not begin to replace the love and personal attention she really needed from them. They had left Ann with an empty emotional tank.

Fortunately, John and Mary worked hard to gain insight into Ann's problem and found ways to share in her life. As Ann heard her parents express their love and concern, and experienced it daily at home, she began to loosen up and communicate with them in a more positive way.

It has been a slow and painful process, but Ann and her parents are truly getting acquainted for the first time. Their sincere desire to develop a loving family is the key to the success of their counseling sessions. Ann's anger has gradually subsided as she has realized that her parents love her. This knowledge, and the feelings of self-worth that Ann is experiencing, will sustain and strengthen her in the trying days ahead.

Taking Ann to church camp, giving her piano lessons, and buying her new clothes all the time in no way filled her emotional needs. She became an angry, frustrated teenager who sought emotional fulfillment outside her home. If John and Mary thought that two hours every Sunday and church camp would fill Ann's spiritual needs, they were wasting their time. She was too angry to accept spiritual teachings, and she was too antiauthority to adopt any attitudes suggested by her parents.

## Do We Really Know Our Children?

Ann's story, with minor changes, typifies far too many of today's families. Parents become so involved in their own problems, in the stress and strain of everyday life, that they forget to stop and talk or listen to their children. As a result, many children are angry and depressed because their emotional needs are not being met.

These young people simply turn outside their homes for need satisfaction. This is not totally undesirable because young people *do* need friends, but if parents are not aware of who these friends are, trouble often rears its ugly head. A damaging involvement in drugs, sex, lying, cheating, or stealing is almost certain for a teen who feels unloved by his parents.

Some statistics might be helpful at this point. According to a recent survey of 8,000 Protestant young people from fifth through ninth grades, 87 percent of the ninth graders believe that Jesus Christ is the Son of God who died on the cross and rose again. Now that's a positive picture, isn't it? Unfortunately, by the time these same young people are eighteen, only 20 percent of them will say they are committed to Christ or will define themselves in any way as Christian. The remaining 80 percent will have lost their faith in the church and the Lord of their parents.

# Will Your Children Carry On Your Faith?

Before World War II, the status of Christianity in Europe was about where the United States is now, maybe even a little stronger. Yet now in England, for example, only 7 percent bother to attend church. The Muslim religion has grown 50 percent in the past five years and is gaining tremendous strength in that country. Many old European church buildings are empty. Some are even being purchased by churches in the United States and rebuilt here.

A study of 20th-century church history indicates that the United States is only a generation behind Europe. One generation ago, Europe was experiencing exactly the same problems with child-rearing that we are today. Their offspring were losing their way to Christ the same as ours are now.

Why is this happening? Why are fewer and fewer young people continuing in the faith? I feel very strongly that the answer lies in the way we are raising our children. We do not really *know* our children. We are not communicating our true feelings to them; we are not letting them know that we love them—unconditionally.

Once you are able to love your child unconditionally, you will be able to guide him successfully to adulthood. Unconditional love is real love. It should exist in *all* love relationships.

## Unconditional Love vs. the Antiauthority Bent

If you love your child unconditionally, you love him *no matter what.* You love him if he is tall or short, fat or skinny, grouchy or happy. In short, you love him no matter what his handicaps, assets, or liabilities. Unconditional love means you love your *child,* but you do not always love his behavior. A perfect definition of unconditional love is given in 1 Corinthians 13:4-7: "Love is patient, love is kind. It does not envy, it does not boast, it is not proud. It is not rude, it is not self-seeking, it is not easily angered, it keeps no record of wrongs. Love does not

15

delight in evil but rejoices with the truth. It always protects, always trusts, always hopes, always perseveres."

Any child who has less than unconditional love from his parents will be an angry, frustrated child. He will not be happy in any area of his life, including the spiritual area.

Let's go back and look at Ann's reaction to feeling unloved. What did she do? She sought love elsewhere and became pregnant. She was angry with her parents and went against them. She also went against their spiritual values. And this is a point I want to emphasize: *spirituality is not something which should be kept separate and apart from all other aspects of your child's life.*

Spirituality is just *one* part of the whole person, and it is very much influenced by the rest of the personality. Your children are physical beings, emotional beings, psychological beings, and spiritual beings. These components are all related, each to the others.

The way you help your child handle anger, frustration, and his natural antiauthority behavior during the teen years will affect him spiritually in exactly the same way it affects him physically, emotionally, and psychologically.

The formulation and the dynamics, the cause and effect, the reasons why teens lapse in faith are exactly the same dynamics, exactly the same situations, and exactly the same reasons why teens have all the other problems in their lives. If your child is antiauthority about academics, about staying out late, about any area in his life, he will be antiauthority about spirituality too. I stress this to all parents who come to me for counseling. If you can keep as much anger as possible out of your child's life, his chances of becoming a strong Christian adult are greatly improved. And the way to keep this anger to a minimum is unconditional love.

The survey mentioned earlier reveals that 54 percent of parents of fifth-graders display little positive physical and verbal attention daily to their children. Only 32 percent of parents of

## Will Your Children Carry On Your Faith?

ninth-graders give their children positive physical and verbal attention. This abrupt drop in affection and nurturance comes just when young adolescents need it most. It comes at a time when they have increasing needs to feel self-confident, and yet, ironically, are instead feeling threats to their self-esteem because their parents pay so little attention to them. Again, look at Ann. She just wanted someone to stop and talk with her for a minute. New designer jeans couldn't fill her emotional tank.

All you need do is pick up any newspaper or watch any television news hour, and you will see that antiauthority attitudes are running rampant in our world today. Divorce, family conflict, a breakdown of moral values—all of these are antiauthority, and all are major influences in the lives of our children. Look at the MTV television channel and you will see the major influences to which teenagers are exposed outside their homes—all antiauthority.

This same antiauthority attitude can show itself in the spiritual life of your child. I repeat: if he is anti-parent, anti-academics, anti-anything, he will also be anti-spiritual. He must have his emotional needs met and feel unconditional love so that he will not develop damaging anger and antiauthority attitudes.

You cannot force your child into accepting spiritual values if he does not feel your love and concern. Many Christian leaders today are telling parents to administer harsh disciplinary actions (e.g., use corporal punishment often) and break the stubborn wills of children who misbehave. The results of such authoritarian teachings are angry children, rebelling from the faith in which they were nurtured.

If this practice continues, the future of Christianity is gloomy. The only way to ensure that the next generation will be Christian is for parents to practice love and spirituality daily in the lives of their children. The children from these homes will want to follow the faith of their parents.

Almost every day, I talk with children and teenagers who are

17

hurting because they do not feel loved. And the sad thing about it all is that Christian parents think they are doing the right thing. They are following the advice of certain Christian child-rearing "experts," but the results are not what they expected.

In their book *What Are They Teaching Our Children?* Mel and Norma Gabler remind us that absolutes are not being taught in public-school curriculum.

The only absolute truth in modern humanistic education is that there are no absolute values. All values must be questioned—especially home- or church-acquired values. Discard the experience gained from thousands of years of Western civilization. Instead, treat the students as primitive savages in the area of values. Let them select their own from slanted, inadequate information. Nothing, absolutely nothing, is certain. There are no universal rules—absolutely none.

Unfortunately, today's society does not provide the standards needed to support our youth. Society does not produce emotional or spiritual growth. This is the sole responsibility of loving, Christian parents with the help of the church. Society's alternatives are less than attractive, as the following counseling episode illustrates.

Glen Andrews, a respected medical doctor, sat slumped in his chair, as though the weight of the world were on his shoulders. "If anybody had told me six months ago that I would be sitting in a psychiatrist's office discussing my son's drug problem, I would have laughed in his face," he said. "I always figured Andy was a pretty good kid. At least he usually seemed happy and contented to me."

Peg Andrews sat next to her husband, folding and refolding her handkerchief. Her face mirrored the pain I knew she was feeling. "Where did we go wrong, Dr. Campbell? Do you think

18

## Will Your Children Carry On Your Faith?

Andy could have a physical problem that caused him to take drugs? Should he have a physical checkup? Could he have inherited a tendency toward using drugs? Oh, I'm so confused. I don't know what to think!"

I turned to Glen. "You said earlier that Andy always seemed happy and never gave you much trouble. Had you noticed any change at all in him before you found he was using drugs?"

"I guess it was about a year ago that I mentioned to Peg that Andy's grades were down a little. It was about that time too that he began to stay in his room a lot. I didn't think much about it. Just thought it was a passing thing. We didn't make any particular issue of it."

"About eight or nine months ago, I noticed that he was running with a different group of friends," Peg added. "They weren't the kind of kids we would have chosen for him, but we didn't want to interfere. We have always prided ourselves in letting Andy make all his own decisions, and that includes choosing friends.

"But in the last two or three months, we've hardly seen him at all. When he *is* in the house, he's in his room. We thought we were raising him in a fair, open-minded way, but since finding those drugs in his room, I wonder if we've done anything right."

Glen dropped his head as Peg fell silent and waited for me to speak. "I tell you what. Why don't I talk with Andy for a while, and then the three of you together can come back into my office. Don't give up; we'll do all we can to get you through this."

Glen and Peg left the room, and I motioned for Andy to come in. He shuffled across the floor, his long, unkempt hair matching his faded, raveled jeans. I managed some small talk for a few minutes, gradually drawing him into a conversation, and then we discussed his use of drugs.

"Why do you think you started using drugs, Andy?" I asked.

"Just bored, I guess," he replied. "Curious. There's nothing

19

much else to do. Nobody at home cares where I am or what I'm doing anyway. They never know or ask where I'm going or who I'm going with or when I'm coming back."

As Andy began to feel comfortable with me, he confided that he would like to spend time with his dad, but his dad was always too busy. "He doesn't want to spend time with me; he has too many more important things to do."

This kind of situation always puzzles me. I know that Glen and Peg are good parents. They have tried to give Andy all the basic needs of life. They have a good marriage. They truly love and respect each other and yet, somewhere along the way, something went wrong. They didn't realize that they had neglected to show or tell Andy that they also loved and respected him.

I met regularly with Glen, Peg, and Andy, and gradually they became aware of the feelings they felt but were unable to show. It will take time for Andy to put things back together, but I have hopes for this family because they are not afraid to ask for help, and they have a basic foundation of love.

## The Bored and Bombarded Generation

I'm a parent too, and I know all the pressures that leave us little time. But I can't stress enough the importance of time spent with your child. When we become too busy to let our kids know how much we love them, we are doing them great harm. If we leave them out of our lives more than we include them, they will become angry, depressed, and bored. It is when they are experiencing these feelings that they become the most vulnerable to negative influences.

In a recent lecture on adolescent drug abuse, Sergeant Bud Hulsey, Youth Officer with the Kingsport, Tennessee Police Department, declared: "I have asked many parents why they think their children get involved with drugs, and I get two

20

answers—peer pressure and escape from reality. But of the 4,000 to 5,000 kids I have asked, not one of them said they take drugs due to peer pressure or for escape. Almost everyone said it was because they were bored, and that they like the feeling—they liked the buzz."

In speaking to youth groups, Sergeant Hulsey tells teens that they are not just physical beings. "You are spiritual beings, emotional beings, intellectual beings, and physical beings. And if you satisfy only your physical being, you are going to be retarded spiritually, emotionally, and intellectually!"

He is so right. But society is screaming at our kids to satisfy their physical desires. Society and parents are standing empty-handed when it comes to helping them grow spiritually, emotionally, or intellectually. So it is up to parents to become aware of these needs and meet them at home. And the first step in doing this is to offer your child unconditional love. Only then will he develop into a whole child; not a bored and depressed teenager, but a self-confident, capable young adult ready to adopt the lifestyle of his parents, including their spiritual values.

Our national morality has reached an all-time low in the last twenty-five years. In that short span, we have heard educators tell teens that their bodies are their own—they can do what they want with them, including having premarital sex. The only precaution is that the people involved should be responsible; pregnancy should be avoided.

Four-letter words are commonplace on television. Sex and obscenity are the norm in movies. These movies used to be prohibited in family theaters, but now they are available to anyone, anywhere.

Teens today are bombarded with information that teens twenty-five years ago hardly knew existed. And with today's economic conditions forcing both parents into the work force, teens are receiving unheard-of freedom and less and less parental guidance.

Kids Who Follow, Kids Who Don't

I know that what I am saying sounds dismal and hopeless, but facts must be faced. The attitudes of today's teenagers, if allowed to continue, will cause an even further decline in church and family life. It is up to us as parents to look deeply into our relationships with our teenaged children. It is up to us to admit our weaknesses, try to understand them, and begin to work toward improvement. A strong, Christ-centered, love-based relationship with our kids will make the difference between Christian and non-Christian adulthood.

I recently attended a conference of leaders in a national youth ministry. I found most pessimistic and disillusioned. Many are leaving the ministry. The general opinion of these leaders was that teens today lack spirit, are depressed, and possess a strong antiauthority attitude. Little progress is being made toward reaching these young people.

These youth leaders felt that most youth groups are made up of kids who are forced to attend church, not by young people who sincerely want to follow their parents' spiritual attitudes and develop spiritual values of their own. Of the teenagers in youth groups, most are junior-high kids—only 5 in 150 are high-school seniors. What are these numbers telling us?

They are saying that we just can't raise our kids like kids were raised twenty-five or thirty years ago. We cannot *make* them go to church, knowing that many will rebel during some of their teen years, and then depend on society to gradually guide them back. The basic moral values are just not out there anymore.

## What's a Christian Parent to Do?
Christian parents are searching for help in developing their children into spiritual adults. The problem is that they are receiving wrong information. Many of today's Christian writers are so overzealous about helping parents get their child into church that they tend to overlook the whole child.

## Will Your Children Carry On Your Faith?

They deal only with disciplining the child about spiritual matters. Parents are told to *force* their children to do their bidding, and all else will fall into place, including spirituality. Exactly the opposite is true. When you *force* a child, you anger him, and an angry child will become antiauthority and will go exactly opposite the desired direction.

Another problem which occurs when parents seek advice about raising children is that they read only what they want to read; they derive from their reading only that information which agrees with their preconceived ideas on the subject. Many parents feel that they already know all there is to know about child-rearing. These are the parents who are difficult to reach. These are the parents who need to honestly question their ideas and weed out those that are unbiblical.

The advice I am offering in this book is based on eighteen years of working with children. It is offered because of my sincere and anxious concern for the future of the church and the family. The sad truth is all around us. Young people are not adopting their parents' spiritual values. They are going in exactly the opposite direction—a direction which is depleting Christianity in the United States today.

A recent Gallup Poll reveals that nine of ten Americans *think* of themselves as Christians; two-thirds say they will spend eternity in heaven. Don't be deceived by these numbers. When these people are asked if they have a personal relationship with Jesus Christ, their answers greatly alter the percentages.

It is up to Christian parents to make that Gallup Poll a Christian reality. It is up to us to guide our children into becoming Christian adults so that nine of ten Americans will not just *think* they are Christians—they will *know* they are Christians. And if you follow the guidelines I set forth in this book, I believe that your child will become an adult who knows he is a Christian.

On a recent television special dealing with teen pregnancies,

23

a doctor made the following statement: "To really combat this terrible problem of teenage pregnancies, we must see to it that the *whole child* is developed. Even before kindergarten, when children are still toddlers at home, parents must see to it that their kids feel loved and respected. Only in this way can these children develop self-esteem. Then and only then will we begin to solve the awesome problem of the teen pregnancy rate of today."

That's the key. We must lovingly help our children develop as whole beings. We cannot zero in on one area of their life, and expect the rest to take care of itself.

The purpose of this book is to guide you through helping your child develop as a whole being, so that when he is a young adult, he will adopt your spiritual values. I suggest that you set a goal of Christian adulthood for your child, and then lovingly guide him toward that end.

It won't be easy. I'm not offering you twelve simple steps to raising spiritual sons and daughters; I'm offering advice to sincere Christian parents who want for their children the meaning and fulfillment which only Christianity can provide.

# 2

# Parent, Know Thyself

*"This is what the Lord Almighty says: 'Give careful thought to your ways'"* (Haggai 1:7).

Knowing who you are and how you feel about yourself plays a very important part in how you interact with your children. Ellen's story, shared just as she told it to me, will enable you to more fully understand the importance of self-knowledge—especially self-esteem.

"I was born into a family of twelve children. It would seem that any parents who already had twelve children would not be particularly pleased about the arrival of the thirteenth, but my parents were not just any parents. I always felt their love and concern for me, so they must have been happy about my arrival.

"My problem didn't develop because I was unloved; it developed because I was so quiet. Oh, I did my share of making noise and I caused my share of arguments. By quiet, I mean I always wanted everyone to be peaceful. I was forever trying to settle disputes which occurred daily in our large household. Even when I was the cause of the argument, I was always the first one to back down—the first one to say, 'Aw, just forget it; it was my fault.'

"For as long as I can remember, I really felt awful if I couldn't settle an argument, if I couldn't restore calm. Sometimes, I would blame myself if one of the other kids got a spanking, thinking, 'If I had tried just a little harder, maybe I could have talked him out of misbehaving.'

"Then another problem attitude developed within me. Maybe it was because I was the baby of the family, but I felt that no one really took me seriously, neither my older brothers and sisters nor my parents. I was just the 'cute little baby sister' and if I didn't complete an assigned task, somebody else would. My parents were probably so glad that I was such an easy kid to get along with that they saw no need to create problems which could easily be avoided. After all, there were plenty of other able bodies around to get things done.

"Anyway, regardless of why it happened, it happened. I gradually began to realize that my actions or lack of actions did not have the same impact as those of my siblings.

"And so I went into adulthood, carrying these odd notions in my mind—feeling worse and worse about not keeping constant peace among my siblings, and feeling less and less that anything I did was important.

"In retrospect, I realize that that was the image I projected to my peers. I was the peacemaker who felt terrible if she failed, but on the other hand, I didn't amount to all that much anyway, so nothing really mattered. That is the way my peers reacted to me. They learned to depend on me to settle arguments, but they walked on me whenever they didn't need a peacemaker, and I let them do it.

"Now, here comes the bad part. I took these attitudes with me into marriage and parenting. When my husband and I disagreed, I would always be the first to want to restore peace. I taught him very quickly that his word was much more important than mine—that I really didn't amount to all that much.

"And our first two children—did I ever do a number on them! Without realizing it, I gave them the 'peace at all costs' and 'low

26

self-esteem' messages, and tried to train them to act the same way. And I topped it all off by setting their dad up as the total authority figure. What a burden I placed on him!

"Our little family struggled along for about twelve years, and then one day I started crying. I knew I had to have professional help.

"It wasn't an overnight thing, but gradually I learned who I was. Then came the tedious task of helping the kids pull out of the mold I had built for them—just as they were going into adolescence. It left some pretty bad scars on the kids, and it almost destroyed my marriage, but we did make it.

"The two older children have now moved away from home, but maybe their little brother will be able to reap some of the benefits of my newly established self-worth. I know for sure that things will be different for him.

"Shortly after he was born, my oldest daughter said, 'You know, Mother, I think God gave T.J. to you and Daddy because He knew all along that you were a good mother. He knew that you would get your thoughts straightened out. But don't you ever worry, you didn't do all that bad with the two of us.'

"I am one of the lucky parents. I finally got acquainted with myself in time to salvage my family and my marriage. I know now that the only way to be an effective parent is to really know and love yourself."

In my years of counseling, I have heard various renditions of Ellen's story. Many times, I have seen how the personal problems of parents can cause serious damage to their children. As a general rule and depending on the personalities of the children, parents with low self-esteem will affect their children negatively, both as they are raising them and when they reach adulthood.

It is extremely important for a mother and father to take an honest look at themselves and discover who they are. Self-confidence and self-worth must be evident at all times so that the children can learn to develop these same traits. And parents must be able to love themselves so that they can give their children the unconditional love so necessary to their full development.

After you have gotten in touch with yourself and have determined whether you are a submissive, quiet person like Ellen (and that's not all bad—it just has to be handled properly) or a more aggressive, "look out world, here I come" person, let's take a look at how you apply yourself in daily life. Place a check mark for each question in the category that best describes you.

| HOME | Always | Sometimes | Rarely |
|---|---|---|---|
| **Married Parents** | | | |
| 1. Do you have and exhibit respect for your mate? | | | |
| 2. If you are both employed, do you share the workload at home? | | | |
| 3. Do you nag and complain about every wrongdoing of your spouse? | | | |
| **Single Parents** | | | |
| 4. Do you constantly belittle your ex-mate to your children? | | | |
| 5. Do you try to feel and show some respect for your ex-mate? | | | |
| 6. Do you have a good attitude about the opposite sex? | | | |
| **WORK** | | | |
| 7. Do you give your employer a full day's work? | | | |

28

| | | | |
|---|---|---|---|
| 8. Do you do as little as possible on the job and then demand full pay? | | | |
| 9. Do you pattern your workday after the axiom, "Anything worth doing is worth doing well"? | | | |
| 10. If you are an employer, are you fair and honest with your employees, giving them the best working conditions possible? | | | |
| **RELIGION** | | | |
| 11. Do you try to cultivate Christianity in your marriage? | | | |
| 12. Do you try to do things *for* God? | | | |
| 13. Do you spend some time every day alone with God? | | | |
| 14. Is your interaction with the general public Christ-centered? | | | |

Honestly answering these questions will help you ascertain your strengths and weaknesses, and then to begin to build the positives and correct the negatives. Remember: all that you do and all that you say are the examples after which your children will pattern their lives. They are either going to want to do the same things you do, or they are going to feel so sorry for the people whom you have mistreated that they will lose their respect and love for you.

It is essential for you as a parent to maintain a positive and optimistic attitude. It is essential that you maintain an attitude of responsibility and fairness, because the very best way to teach a child is by example. If you are constantly pessimistic and exhibit negative, irresponsible behavior, you are promoting an antiauthority lifestyle to your children. You are showing them that they don't have to be responsible for their actions. Teenagers constantly influenced by antiauthority parents are placed in double jeopardy because they are already, by nature, antiauthority.

## The Question of Divorce

It is very difficult to make a generalized statement about divorce. However, in most cases, if the parents will try to work out their problems, the children are far better off. In well over 80 percent of the cases I have seen, I have strongly encouraged both partners to try to resolve their marital difficulties.

Let's get back to Ellen's story. Now, there is a marriage that could easily have ended in divorce. But counseling revealed that Ellen and her husband had too much to lose to separate. They had two fine children and a lot of respect for each other even though Ellen had some serious problems to work through. I encouraged them to wait until Ellen got a handle on things before they made up their minds about getting a divorce.

Obviously, both partners in that marriage worked very hard to resolve the problems. I was glad that they took my advice and gave it some time. They now have a great marriage, and their family has increased by a son, a son-in-law, and a beautiful granddaughter.

However, there are marriages in which one partner is so sick that the other is in danger. In these cases, I do not recommend reconciliation. My main consideration is to offer support and help on an individual basis.

Unfortunately, in many marriages, the basic problem is selfishness. And no wonder, for the prevailing attitude of today is "me-ism." What's more, the absence of moral values in society makes it very easy to become involved with someone else and simply walk out of a marriage.

Many couples get married because they have low self-esteem, thinking the marriage will solve the problem. The fact is, just the opposite occurs, because it takes an awful lot of "self" to make a marriage work.

For a while, Ellen's marriage contained only one confident self, and that was her husband. It must have been very frustrating for him to be the only real partner in a marriage of two people. An ideal marriage is a union of two strong, self-confident people who know themselves and exhibit their feelings from the onset of the relationship.

Getting to know yourself and developing high self-esteem will help you to look at any problem from a different point of view. If, for example, your marriage is in trouble, an honest, different view of the situation could just put it on the road to recovery.

Craig Reid sat defiantly across from me, his body slightly turned away from his wife, Fran. They were both bright young people, but they were seriously considering a divorce.

"I have my work and a couple of interesting hobbies," Craig said. "Fran never wants to do anything with me. She just stays home with the kids. We don't have anything in common anymore. I keep telling her that she can get a weekend sitter for the kids and we can go boating or climbing. We can afford it. She works too."

"And I keep telling him that we don't have much time to spend with the kids as it is," Fran interrupted. "I think he is being just plain selfish. Not only does he want to do just what he enjoys, he insists that I do what he enjoys too. After working all week, I need a little time just for me, and the kids need us too."

Fran turned directly toward her husband. "Craig, you are a very selfish person. I wish we could all go climbing together once in a while. I could stay in the foothills with the boys while you go on to the top, and we could be waiting for you when you

31

return. I am so tired of saying no to you, and watching you storm out of the house never considering why I said no. And then you come home on Sunday evenings and don't bother to tell us anything about your weekend.

"We'll be better off without you because we won't have to look forward to those hateful homecomings you always give us."

"Craig," I interjected, "how do you feel about being called selfish? Do you see yourself as a selfish person?"

"No. I never thought I was selfish. I make a good living and give Fran and the boys a lot. I don't think that's being selfish. I even ask Fran to come along with me. Is that selfish?"

"But I want to include the boys. They're old enough now to be with us, and they need us. That's the part I've never been able to get you to understand." Fran seemed to be pleading now. "Craig, you give plenty of things to them, but so little of yourself. I just can't stand to see them hurt anymore." Fran covered her face with her hands and cried.

"Fran, don't cry. You know I hate it when you cry. Why didn't you tell me all of this before? Why didn't you tell me the boys needed me? I thought they had all they needed. They have you, and I'm home once in a while."

"I never could get you to listen until now. Now that we're sitting here in Dr. Campbell's office where I can talk without you yelling at me, I finally feel brave enough to tell you how I feel."

"Is Fran being honest, Craig?" I asked. "Do you yell at her and refuse to listen to her suggestions?"

Craig fell back in his chair. "I guess she's right, Dr. Campbell. I don't pay much attention when she tries to rearrange my weekends. I usually just slam out of the house. I don't like to have people telling me what to do and what not to do with my time."

It took a few months of counseling, but Craig acquired a different perspective of himself. Often a third party can be the answer; that's why it's good to seek professional help when you have problems. Craig and Fran were able to sort out a lot of little things that had been bothering them. I felt all along that theirs was a marriage that could be saved. It just needed a different point of view. I am happy to report that even the boys do a little hill climbing with their dad now.

A troubled marriage is very damaging to children, who usually experience problems with their ability to think rationally, logically, and sequentially because of the troubled home front. As a consequence, their grades go down. Craig and Fran's boys were experiencing these things. They were fighting with their friends. In time, their spirituality would have suffered because even spirituality requires the possession of a certain amount of logic to be understood.

A marriage based on Jesus Christ is a beautiful, strong marriage. Craig and Fran now have that marriage. Obedience to Christ in a marital relationship means a lifelong, selfless commitment to each other and the children of that marriage.

When we put the needs of our spouse and our children before our own desires, our needs are met by God and family members. It is a beautiful circle. No marriage is always easy and perfect, but when problems do arise, a Christian marriage has the power of God at its disposal.

This kind of home offers much for the children to copy and carry into their own homes as adults. They will easily learn by example how to make Christ the center of the household. Preaching, threatening, and demanding will not be necessary, because the child from this home will want to follow parental examples.

## The Things We Teach Our Children

Later in this book, I will devote an entire chapter to discipline, but here I want to make a point about teaching a child right from wrong.

There is a big difference between discipline and education. Discipline is used in determining a child's behavior, while education deals with morality. A child cannot be disciplined in morality; he must be taught morality by word and by example. In other words, you must teach a child what is right and what is wrong; you do not discipline him into it.

This is one area in which you should really know yourself and give careful thought to your ways. It is the one in which parents make the most flagrant mistakes, causing their children to rebel against parental ideas of right and wrong. Parents try all too often to *discipline* their children instead of educating them by example.

When children are punished for the wrong reasons and under wrong conditions, they rebel. They have to see proper behavior lived out before their eyes before they can understand and copy it. The sad fact is that far too many parents follow the old axiom, "Do as I say, not as I do," and then don't understand why their children rebel against what they say.

It is hard to educate your children in matters of right and wrong if you are doing one thing and saying another. How can parents hope to instill any kind of values in their children, including spiritual values, if they are having affairs, writing bad checks, doing lousy work for their employers, being deceitful, cheating—in short, doing what far too many people are doing today? Look at the parent who cheats on his income tax returns every year, and then becomes totally irate when he finds that his child has cheated on a test at school. What a confused kid! He was just doing what his father taught him to do.

And what in the world is this same kid going to do about spirituality if his parents preach it, but don't live it? Probably very little. I think Titus 1:16 aptly describes the situation: "They claim to know God, but by their actions they deny Him."

It is the action of denial that your children will copy. The verbal demands that you make in trying to discipline them into a Christian lifestyle will only create in them feelings of rebellion and confusion, and will move them away from Christianity. What you speak must come from your heart and be evident in your daily life.

## Is Our Christianity Showing?

Let's go back to the test at the beginning of this chapter and discuss the section on religion. What is your attitude toward God? Spending time with Him each day—not a rigid, set time, but a quiet, unscheduled time to be alone with Him and get to know Him—is a must for every Christian.

And the people with whom you come in contact every day—waitresses, bank tellers, store clerks, people to whom you can be nice or not nice—is your interaction with them Christ-centered? Do you try to present Christ to them by the way you treat them, not necessarily in witnessing, but at least in your attitude toward them?

How do you interact with the leaders in your church? Do you sit in church Sunday after Sunday and tune out the sermon? Your mind drifts to thoughts of why the building committee didn't take your advice. Or why the ushers don't make the building cooler. And then, do you take these concerns home and discuss them in a negative way at Sunday dinner? Do you criticize other Christians?

Again, all these things are examples to your children. And since they pertain directly to the church, they will have a strong influence on the way your children view Christianity. So it is imperative that you become completely honest about how you feel about your own spirituality, and correct the areas which are detrimental to both your children and yourself.

We all go through phases in our spiritual growth. When we first become Christians, we are excited and on fire for the Lord.

35

We experience strong, vibrant emotions because we feel so good. This is the time we are wide open for teaching, and we grow by leaps and bounds in our Christian knowledge.

Then we enter what I call the "either-black-or-white phase." We become very rigid and feel that everything pertaining to our faith has to be only one way—either totally black or totally white. This is a stage of spiritual immaturity, but everyone goes through it. It's like learning how to drive a car.

In fact, this learning pattern—dealing first with the concrete realities and then with the "gray areas"—is true in almost all phases of life, but few people apply it to their spirituality. As we mature and learn that choices are not always black and white, and exact answers are not always available, one of two things will happen. We either learn to become more reasonable and flexible in our thinking without losing our faith, or we lose our faith.

More and more people today are simply rejecting their faith. In our counseling practice, my colleagues and I are seeing fewer and fewer people over the age of forty-five who are still practicing Christians. And if they are Christians, they are not growing spiritually. Many have become discouraged because the rigid things, the pat answers they learned during their either-black-or-white stage do not always apply to all of life's experiences.

A perfect example of this is trying to cope with the complexities of raising teenagers. There are simply no nice, pat answers for every problem that arises.

Try to determine your current phase of spiritual growth. If you are still in the rigid phase, you will adversely affect your children, especially if you have a tendency to be unbending when dealing with them. One of the most important traits a parent, especially of teenagers, must possess is flexibility. Flexibility does not mean permissiveness. It means not being rigid in your expectations, but remaining pleasant, positive, and firm as you guide your children in the decision-making process.

# Parent, Know Thyself

For example, one young mother recently told me how proud she was that all three of her daughters were taking dancing lessons. "I absolutely insisted that they all take dancing," she said. "I took ballet and I want the same for my children. I think it's important for their physical well-being, plus it's very character-building." Unfortunately, she didn't ask the girls if they really wanted to dance.

I just happened to know that the oldest one wanted to take swimming lessons instead, but went dutifully to dance class every Saturday morning. How much happier this girl would have been if she could have been dropped off at the pool while her sisters danced. But the mother wasn't flexible. She had made up her mind that all of her daughters would take dancing lessons, and that's what they did.

Chances are this is not a particularly happy home. It is most likely a home where Mother "rules the roost." And that is unfortunate, for above all we must make our homes havens for our children. They must be places where our sons and daughters feel secure, relaxed, and loved. It is very hard for a parent in the either-black-or-white phase of his spirituality to achieve such an atmosphere.

When many Christians emerge from the either-black-or-white stage and realize no absolute answers exist for most problems, they are faced with the danger of becoming cynical. They may see a Christian hero perform a non-Christian act. They begin to realize that living a Christian life is difficult. They see that they must use their own minds to think, and that they must spend time with the Lord and daily ask for His leading.

The danger at this point is that one can become very disillusioned. Unfortunately, this occurs for most parents about the same time that their kids are teenagers—the time when their kids need the most stability in their lives. And here we are as parents, having a hard time with many of our own thoughts and beliefs. It is during times like these that we must hang ferociously to our faith. Remember the words of Solomon: "My son, do not forget my teaching, but keep my commands in your heart, for they will prolong your life many years and bring you prosperity" (Proverbs 3:1-2).

We must seek time to pray, to read Scripture and, above all, we must not let the mistakes, lies, and frailties of other Christians undermine our spiritual foundations. I have seen that happen again and again. Whatever the inner turmoils, we must be careful not to show a visible, cynical attitude toward spirituality at this time, because it will be directly reflected in our children.

During these episodes when we feel our faith is weakening, we should step back and review our spiritual life as it was during the either-black-or-white stage. We should try to grasp some of the positive attitudes we had then, and hang on until our feelings of cynicism weaken and our spirituality becomes strong again.

It is sort of like saying, "Stop the world; I'd like to step off for a few minutes and get a different view of life." Or it's like stepping out of the cloudy water and letting the mud settle to the bottom. Soon you'll be able to see things clearly again.

Don't worry; it is perfectly normal for your teenagers to see you struggle, as long as you don't choose antiauthority, cynical solutions to your problems. Adopting that kind of attitude will immediately kill the spiritual growth of your children. They need to see you working toward positive, biblical solutions to your problems.

The same advice applies to a troubled marriage. As long as your children see that you are struggling to improve the situation, they will have hope and will not be damaged. The damage occurs when cynicism overrides the struggle for improvement and a constant state of turmoil develops.

When you finally get through this difficult phase of your spirituality, you then enter your spiritual adolescence. It's a real questioning time in your life. You question churches and, in a healthy way, question your own faith. This is real growth.

It is healthy to question your authorities and what has been handed down to you through the years. Sometimes, when you get into thoughtful examination, you find that some of your presuppositions are wrong. I found, for example, that God does not have a detailed, pinpointed plan for my life. Instead, His plan for my life is based on my own decision making, as I seek to prayerfully follow His leading.

This is the time when you really begin to find out things on your own. You begin reading Scripture with a new light. You begin interpreting it against your own experiences, and not the experiences of others. Be careful, though, for there is a danger in this phase.

The danger is that we tend to forget that our children have not gone through this or any other phase of Christianity. If you try to explain your attitude toward your spiritual life to your children now, you will really confuse them. Incidentally, this holds true in relating to other newer Christians as well.

So, what you must do is make your spiritual attitudes continually obvious to your children in your daily life. Again, I stress, I know these suggestions are not always easy, but I do know that they will pay off in the long run for both you and your children.

And so, if you always give careful thought to your ways, and present them in a Christ-centered manner, you are giving your best to your children. Equally as important as getting to know yourself, and giving careful thought to how you present yourself, is getting to know your children. I don't just mean that you should recognize their appearance and the sound of their voice; I mean you must get to know your children as whole individuals. Understanding each child's specific personality is of the utmost importance. Let's discuss this next.

# 3

# Twenty-five Percenters

*"See that you do not look down on one of these little ones.
For I tell you that their angels in heaven always see the
face of My Father in heaven. In the same way your
Father in heaven is not willing that any of these little ones
should be lost" (Matthew 18:10, 14).*

If I had to tell you that you could read only two chapters in this
book, I would choose this one and the next. I would choose
these two chapters, because becoming totally aware of your
child's personality is the most crucial thing you can do in order
to help him develop into a strong Christian adult.

I have found it practical to separate people by the way they
respond to authority, and place them into two categories—
approximately 25 percent are basically pro-authority; about 75
percent are generally antiauthority (i.e., they usually consider
their own opinions above those of others).

I have two sons, David and Dale. Dale is my 25 percenter and
David is my 75 percenter. Dale was born asking, "Dad, is there
anything you and Mom would like for me to do?" and David
arrived with an order to all in hearing distance: "Would you
people please step out of the way; I have a life to live, and I
would like to get on with it with as little interference as
possible!"

However, nobody is perfect. Each of the boys has his pros and
cons, and each possesses a little of the good and the bad, which

40

offers both problems and joys in raising them. These next two chapters will be a discussion of 25 percenters and 75 percenters.

## The Personality Factor

Every kid in the world is born with a unique personality. Parents can damage that person or enhance his development, but his basic personality is congenital. That is to say, the parents did not create the personality *after* the child was born. They supplied the genetic traits upon conception, and the personality developed from there.

Now, considering that there are millions of people in the world, the fact that I place them into only two categories may surprise you. However, after working with parents and children for about twenty years, I have found that this procedure is both legitimate and practical.

I realize this sounds too simple, but just imagine memorizing all the different characteristics of each type of personality, and trying to apply them, all sorted out, on a minute-by-minute, day-by-day basis. It would be utterly impossible. So, I am offering the practical simplification of describing two basic facets of personalities. I have used this in raising my own children, and also in professionally working with children. *I want to stress again that I don't consider either facet all good or all bad; I just recognize that they exist.*

Basically, how a child responds to almost anything depends on his attitude toward authority, and his attitude toward authority depends on his personality. So, dividing personalities in just two groups is of tremendous value when dealing with the problems of children.

I have shared this division of personalities with many people, and it has worked as beautifully for them as it does for me. When we understand the personalities of our children, we can better understand our children's behavior and emotions, and

41

possibly keep from making some tragic mistakes in raising them. Of course, we are only human. Regardless of the amount of information we gather in an effort to do a perfect job of child-rearing, we are still going to make mistakes. So don't feel guilty when things go wrong, because all that God expects of you is your best, not infallibility.

## What's a 25 Percenter Like?

Twenty-five percenters are born with a need to be under authority. They want approval and praise. They want somebody to tell them what to do and to structure their time for them. They want someone to make decisions for them. So, to the casual observer, the 25 percenter would seem to be an easy child to raise. All you have to do is tell him what to do, set the time for him to do it, tell him when to quit doing it, and then praise him for doing it.

Sounds simple, doesn't it? Well, it's not. Twenty-five percenters are just as difficult to raise as 75 percenters. Where the 75 percenters strike out on their own and begin thinking for themselves almost from day one, the 25 percenters have to be taught to think for themselves. They love to follow; therefore, they are subject to joining cults, to being used, and to not being able to stand on their own two feet as adults. In fact, they have a terrible handicap as adults, because they are always expecting somebody else to tell them what to do.

Twenty-five percenters can be easily controlled with guilt, because they are so prone to guilt. Most parents of 25 percenters control their children in exactly this manner without realizing it, and then take great pride in the fact that they have such wonderfully disciplined children.

Julie Hyde, fourteen-year-old daughter of Evelyn and Richard Hyde, is a perfect example of a 25 percenter controlled by guilt. And Evelyn and Richard are not even aware they are doing it.

Julie is the oldest of the five Hyde children. She is a quiet, obedient 25 percenter. A few weeks ago, a friend invited her to a swimming party. "Mom, Carla is having a swimming party this afternoon and evening and wants me to come. Is it all right with you?"

"Oh, I'm sorry, Julie. I had planned to shop downtown this afternoon and then have dinner with your dad. I was looking forward to it. I had hoped you could watch your brothers and sisters for me. Oh, well, never mind. I'll do it another time."

Julie knew that her mother rarely got out of the house, but she really wanted to go to that swimming party. However, she would have felt terrible being the one to keep her mom from some much-needed time away from the kids. "Go ahead, Mom. My swimsuit's faded anyway. I'd rather wait until I get a new one before I go to a swimming party. Why don't you go on and meet Daddy for dinner. I can stay here."

It began to be easy for Evelyn Hyde to ask her eldest daughter to baby-sit the children, because Julie never complained. She was so convincing that her mom thought she actually enjoyed it. And she did once in a while, but there were many times when she would have liked to have done anything but stay home with her brothers and sisters. It was her guilt that kept her home.

When 25 percenters are very young, they're really neat kids; they are so easy to manage. And the parents of these kids are envied, especially in church and especially by parents of 75 percenters. Parents of 25 percenters are usually overheard saying to parents of 75 percenters: "If you would just become more firm with your child, he would be just like mine."

All parents compare their children, not realizing they simply cannot compare a 25 percenter and a 75 percenter. As a consequence, many children are damaged by this seemingly innocent action of comparison.

Parents who are controlling their children with guilt, as Evelyn and Richard Hyde did Julie, are controlling them in the worst way possible. Even though such control is totally unintentional, it still occurs. Twenty-five percenters are so eager to please that they are easily crushed. They take everything too personally and too seriously. Imagine how Julie would have felt at the swimming party. She would have had a terrible time, because she would have felt personally responsible for denying her mother a pleasurable afternoon and evening.

Twenty-five percenters are always afraid they are going to hurt someone or do something wrong. They are perfectionists, and want to do everything exactly right. Even a bit of criticism will smash their egos and make them feel so guilty that they cannot develop into their own persons.

The parents of very young 25 percenters do not see this. These mothers and fathers just enjoy having a nice little kid who always does exactly what he is told to do, never giving anyone a hard time.

What these parents don't realize is that 25 percenters are keeping all their feelings to themselves. They are extremely self-critical. Being perfectionists doesn't mean that they expect everything to be perfect. It just means that they expect everything to be much better than they, in reality, can make it.

A 25 percenter has such high expectations of himself that every day is a disappointment to him, because every day something goes wrong. Even if ninety-nine good things happen and one bad, he will see only the bad thing. Such a child is obviously prone to depression.

A typical day for a 25 percenter might go something like this: Brett is fifteen and a sophomore in high school. He started this particular day by making an A on his math test and an A on an English test. At this point, he is feeling great. Then he is handed a book report—another A. What a day!

That afternoon, he hits a home run which scores the winning run for his baseball team. After walking home from school, he discovers a note from his mom on the kitchen table. She's shopping and won't be home until 6 o'clock. Never mind—he has to go bowling anyway. He can tell her later about his perfect day.

He goes to his closet and reaches for his red bowling shirt, but it's not there. Then he discovers it in the laundry basket with streaks and stains. His mother didn't wash it. His day is ruined. His team is bowling in a tournament, and he doesn't have his shirt! Everything good about the day leaves Brett.

This story may sound extreme, but this is the way a 25 percenter can think. He can very easily become depressed over one seemingly insignificant happening. And depression causes anger. Keeping in mind that a 25 percenter wants above all to please, he will keep that anger inside, causing even deeper depression. And deeper depression causes more anger, which the 25 percenter is directing inward, toward himself.

Just look at the plight of the 25 percenter when his parents are not aware of his personality. He suffers from years of guilt manipulation. He has not been taught how to think for himself or express his feelings outwardly and verbally. As a consequence, he is going to be a depressed and angry adult.

The natural need of all humans to be loved and feel self-worth is multiplied in the 25 percenter personality. So, when his parents do not realize his low self-esteem and unintentionally leave him with an empty emotional tank, he goes outside his home for need satisfaction.

By the time he becomes a teenager, he may become involved with drugs, lying, cheating, stealing, and sex. The list of all the pain a 25 percenter can cause himself and his parents is endless.

## The Story of Denise

Tall, slender Denise came to see me about eight months ago. A nursing student in her early twenties, her expression gave away her depression. She sat fidgeting in a chair in my office, trying to find the words to discuss her problem with me.

Finally, she blurted it out. "I'm anorexic, Dr. Campbell. I attended a lecture on anorexia this afternoon, and it made me realize that I am anorexic and bulemic." She began to cry. "I don't want to tell my parents because they don't think I've done much of anything right in my life as it is. Now they'll be sure to hate me when they hear this."

I looked into her tear-filled brown eyes. "What are you doing that makes you think you are anorexic, Denise?"

"Well, I starve myself for as long as I can stand it. Then I eat everything in sight, take a laxative, and purge."

"How long have you been doing this?"

"About four months, now, I think."

I was glad to see that Denise recognized her problem as early as she did. She had not yet reached the point of physical damage, so I felt we had a good chance of helping her through it. What we needed to discover was why she felt so negative about herself that she would hurt herself in this way.

As I began to counsel Denise, her problem unfolded. Her older brother, Bill, was outgoing and aggressive. Denise was the quiet one.

"Ever since I can remember, Bill had Mom's or Dad's attention about something," Denise began. "When he was about seven years old, he developed a very serious, life-threatening illness. I stayed with my grandparents while he was in the hospital. I really got lonesome there, but I hated to bother Mom and Dad because I knew that they were upset about Bill.

"Finally, when Bill came home from the hospital, he had to stay in bed for a month. I did everything I could to make him happy. I was glad that we were all home together, but I remember that Mom hardly noticed me. I don't remember feeling that she should notice me, because I knew Bill needed her so much, but I realize now that I did miss her attention.

"When Bill and I were eight and ten, Mom and Dad built a new house. That was really a hectic time. Once, Bill and I got into a fight. We were arguing about some work that Mom had asked us to do. Actually the fight happened when Bill began to tell me what to do. I already knew what to do; Mom had told me. So I punched him in the stomach. He hit me back—right in the mouth—and cut my lip. I really got mad then, and grabbed for his hair. Just as I got a big handful of hair, he jerked away, leaving me with a wad of his hair in my hand.

"Dad came in about then, and took us both to the back porch and spanked us. Afterward, Bill ran out into the backyard, but I came back into the house and finished the job that Mom had asked us to do. I was so scared. I was afraid that Bill would have a bald spot on his head that would never grow back."

So went Denise's life. She told me that she almost always gave in—not just to her brother and her parents, but to anyone who crossed her. However, when she started to high school, she changed.

"Oh, I still tried to keep peace at home, but I was a real character at school. When I was a junior, I went out with a boy who didn't amount to anything. He was just plain trouble. I didn't tell Mom and Dad that I was going out with him, but they found out. Boy, was I in trouble. They lectured me for two weeks. I never went out with that kid again. I didn't know what in the world Mom and Dad would do to me if I did it the second time.

"Again, I felt very guilty because I did something that displeased my parents so. I thought I was probably the worst person in the world."

Denise went from high school to college and failed college. "I made fair grades my first year, but after that I failed everything. I didn't even attend classes. I lied to Mom and Dad, telling them that my grade report must have been lost in the mail.

"I was feeling worse and worse, but I didn't know how to get out of it. Then one day, Mom surprised me and came to visit me at school. She and I visited all my instructors, and I tried to

47

make them all think that I had been attending classes; they just had been negligent in marking my attendance.

"Finally, I couldn't stand it any longer. I broke down and cried and cried and told Mom the truth. I hadn't been attending classes; I had just been hanging around campus goofing off. Mom didn't yell at me. She just called Dad, and he came down with the truck and moved me home. They told me I would have to get a job and pay them back the money I had wasted on my education, or lack of education, as the case was.

"I held two or three different jobs, finally succeeding in paying back the money, but feeling worse and worse about myself. I had no particular direction. I never completed anything I started. Even a relationship I developed with a man who asked me to marry him failed.

"All this time, Mom was directing my life. I didn't think she had done such a great job with her own life, and I resented her interference in mine. But I couldn't afford to move away from home, so I had to put up with her direction.

"When I told her that I was going to finish my education, she was genuinely pleased and offered to loan me the money. I refused the loan. I knew that I was either going to have to do something on my own soon, or I never would. So I borrowed the money and moved out of my parents' house and started back to school.

"I fell into the same old trap of trying to settle everybody's arguments. I felt I was always there for everyone else, but they never seemed to be there for me. I even had one friend who wouldn't let me tell her about my dates because she hadn't been dating. I didn't want her to feel bad, so I didn't tell her. I gave no thought to what I was denying myself.

"As time for graduation drew closer and closer, I panicked. I had never completed anything of importance before, and I was afraid I probably wouldn't complete this.

"I had always been slightly overweight (at least I thought I

48

was), so I started on a diet about the same time that I was beginning to panic about graduation. And soon I discovered that I could lose weight easily—at last I was doing something right! The only problem was that it became an obsession with me."

After about six weeks of intensive counseling with Denise, she began to understand what kind of person she was—a 25 percenter. Being a 25 percenter didn't make her hopeless. Twenty-five percenters are wonderful people. It's just that Denise's 25 percent-personality was not recognized by her parents, and they hadn't interacted with her accordingly.

Just think of the suffering Denise and her parents could have avoided if they had understood her personality. Her parents always loved her. They just didn't realize that her quiet ways were, in essence, deceiving. She didn't demand any attention; as a consequence, she didn't get any extra attention. Her parents just assumed her emotional tank was full, and tended instead to the natural demands of her 75-percenter brother, Bill.

Fortunately, the story of Denise has a happy ending. She graduated third in her class, and is now working in a large hospital in the Midwest. She and her parents have a real relationship these days. It is based on love and understanding and knowledge. Her parents now realize that just because she is quiet and demands little attention doesn't mean she needs no attention from them.

You can see how simple it was for Denise's parents to control her. She wanted approval and praise, so she tried to be the perfect little girl. But it finally became more than she could handle. Her lack of emotional fulfillment resulted in anger and frustration which turned inward, and manifested itself as anorexia.

And what about Denise's spirituality? As an adolescent, Denise attended church and youth meetings and made a profession of faith in Christ as her Saviour. She became the exemplary

49

kid, but as soon as she reached her junior year of high school, she rejected her spiritual training, considering it "baby stuff." However, she kept attending church because she wanted the approval of her parents, and *they* wanted her to attend.

We must be very careful about the spiritual lives of our 25 percenters, but in the process not ignore their emotional, physical, and psychological health. We must recognize the times when they feel anger and teach them to express it openly. We must keep their emotional tanks filled with unconditional love, especially during the antiauthority period so natural to the teenage years. By doing these things, we can be assured that our quiet, little 25 percenters will mature into strong, healthy adults who love the Lord as we do.

# 4

# Seventy-five Percenters

*"Peacemakers who sow in peace raise a harvest of righteousness" (James 3:18).*

I knew when David was about two that he was a 75 percenter. He was definitely one of those "I'd-rather-do-it-myself" children, and I knew how I was going to have to handle him. We've never had to wonder whether or not David was angry; he has always been able to let us know, but Dale, our 25 percenter, is different. My wife, Pat, and I try to be watchful and help Dale to express his anger when we know something is bothering him. Again, I reiterate, this doesn't make one boy better than the other; it just means that we sometimes handle situations differently, depending on the personality involved.

Seventy-five percenters want to do their own thinking. They want to make their own decisions. They want to learn the hard way and to control their own behavior. They can become angry when someone tries to tell them what to do. They feel that if they are going to learn anything at all, they are going to have to do it themselves.

On the surface, the 75 percenter appears much harder to raise than the 25 percenter, but he is not. Even though he is born with an antiauthority attitude (not necessarily grossly

51

antiauthority, just generally antiauthority), he takes the same amount of patience, love, and understanding as the 25 percenter.

He may seem more difficult because he already has an inborn desire to think for himself, and he is going to practice that desire and develop it over the years. That is a God-given talent. It is the reason that 75 percenters are natural leaders.

It is a lot easier to keep your thumb on the 75 percenter and help him keep his behavior under control than it is to teach the 25 percenter how to think on his own. It is so much easier just to tell a kid what to do than it is to teach him how to think.

However, don't come down too hard on a 75 percenter while working with behavior control, because you can make him angry too. A 25 percenter becomes angry because of accumulated guilt, while a 75 percenter won't be hurt at the moment, but will develop a "get even" attitude toward you which will eventually surface.

## Too Many Indians, Not Enough Chiefs

Most Christians, I think, tend to be 25 percenters. This is a critical fact. The church is more likely to lose the 75 percenters, and these are the people who are our natural leaders. There is nothing wrong with 25 percenters, but we can't do without 75 percenters in the church.

Right now, the church has too many Indians and not enough chiefs. Because there are so few 75 percenters in the church, when one does show up, he automatically becomes a leader. This can hurt the church because we don't have enough 75 percenters to achieve a balance. Any leader who has no competition or feedback listens only to himself and gets more and more caught up in his own ideas.

This helps explain why so many churches teach extremely authoritarian doctrine. Today's leaders are leaning in that direction and teaching it as law to the 25 percenters in the congregation. And they are seldom questioned.

For example, most Christians can question what the Apostle Paul and the Apostle Peter mean in their epistles. They can even question what some of Christ's statements mean. But they don't dare question today's 75-percenter, national Christian leaders about *their* thinking.

The danger of all this is that most of these leaders advocate the same thing about raising children and teenagers. They say that the primary way of relating to a child is by disciplining him, especially by beating him with the rod. Such child-rearing theories are a backlash against the "do-your-own-thing" parental passivity of the '60s. And child-rearing at this end of the pendulum means rigid, forceful discipline. Verses in Proverbs dealing with authoritarian discipline are used as proof texts for this school of thought, but they are used with no balance. Nor does this school of thought mention that the shepherd's rod referred to in Scripture was used almost exclusively for *guiding* the sheep, not beating them, as Psalm 23:4 ("Your rod and Your staff, they comfort me") clearly shows.

In my judgment, this misguided teaching is one of the main reasons why so many 75 percenters turn against the church. By the time they are seventeen or eighteen, they are still angry because of their authoritarian upbringing. So, the last place you are going to see them is in church.

The 25 percenter, on the other hand, is more likely to make a commitment to Christ and join the church regardless of how he's treated, because he needs to be under authority.

We are losing the 75 percenter to the temptations of today's "me-first" lifestyle. We are losing him to this lifestyle because it has a built-in antiauthority flavor, and anyone who has enough anger left in him beyond the normal period of adolescence will have an antiauthority attitude and align himself with antiauthority movements.

## An Illustration from the Campbell Household

"I'm not going to church today," thirteen-year-old David stated flatly one Sunday morning a few years ago.

"Oh, come on, David," I replied. "You know that once you get there, you have a good time."

David gave in and went with us. He didn't say anymore about it for three or four weeks. And then again, out of the blue, he announced, "I'm not going to church today. I told you before that I didn't want to go, so I'm not going."

This time I could see that it was useless to talk David into going. He was so determined about the matter that forcing him would have created a destructive antichurch, anti-spiritual attitude that could be extremely difficult to reverse. I had to handle this crisis without alienating David, and yet keep him on the long road to maturity.

"Do you like Sunday School?" I asked.

"Yeah, I don't mind Sunday School."

"OK, I'll tell you what we'll do. You go to Sunday School and your mother and I will take turns taking you home during church and stay home with you."

David agreed to the concept. Pat's and my strategy here was to prevent that vicious anger toward spiritual things which can develop when church attendance or spiritual matters are forced. Knowing that David is a 75 percenter, which makes him naturally antiauthority, we chose for the moment not to pressure him and lose him from the church permanently. We didn't feel we were being permissive; we had a plan.

After all, David was almost fourteen. He knew what we thought and how we believed. He probably knew us better than we knew ourselves. This new arrangement went on for about four or five weeks, and then I could see it was getting old for David. He could tell that Pat and I were really suffering because of it.

He knew that we both wanted to be in church together, that

54

we needed to be in church, so finally he said, "Oh, all right, I'll go to church for your sake." And that was that.

Now this worked for the Campbells. I can't promise that it will work for the parents of every 75 percenter. It depends a great deal on what kind of an overall relationship you have with your child in other areas of his life, not just the spiritual area. If you really get acquainted with your child and trust your instincts, you'll be able to handle your particular situation. The key is to keep things positive, and try not to become too authoritarian with your 75 percenter.

The same principle applies to your 25 percenter, but even more so. He is so prone to guilt, that a strong, negative, authoritarian attitude can really damage his ability to think and make decisions.

## Those Anti-Everything Kids
Now let me tell you about a very sophisticated, self-reliant, middle-aged 75 percenter who just this year found Christ.

Jane is definitely a 75 percenter, born to a very definite 75-percenter mother. As a little girl, she constantly exhibited her antiauthority nature. But her mother kept the upper hand, and would almost always see to it that Jane did exactly as she was told. Fortunately, Jane's best friend attended her church, so she enjoyed Sunday School and tolerated church, sitting defiantly, but nonetheless sitting, beside her mother.

When she became a teenager, she openly rebelled against going to church, but again, her mother won out and saw to it that Jane not only went to church, but that she earned perfect attendance awards.

Jane was a rebellious teenager. She was antiacademics, antichurch; she was antiauthority in general. She was very antisocial and made only one or two friends. When she moved away from her hometown and entered college (the college of her mother's choice), she quit going to church altogether. She even adopted the belief that Jesus Christ was nothing more than a "Good Guy." She vigorously denied the Virgin Birth, claiming it to be simply a myth. She was determined to go in exactly the opposite direction of her mother.

Jane made good enough grades in college to graduate with a degree in nursing, and immediately went to work in her chosen field in a large metropolitan hospital where she met and married a doctor. This marriage produced two children, but ended in a bitter divorce.

During these years of working and child-rearing, she rarely visited her parents. When she did, she spent most of her vacation arguing with her mother.

After her divorce, she met and married quiet, steady Fred. He offered her sons, who now were teenagers, all the love and support he could give them. He was patient with Jane's angry, anti-everything nature.

Fred encouraged Jane to try to develop some kind of a positive relationship with her parents, especially her mother. And so, again she tried to communicate with her mother.

During one of these visits back to her hometown, a visit when she was attempting to heal some of the wounds of the past, Jane shared this realization with a longtime friend: "You know, just before we came to Mother's, my oldest son came to me feeling very down. He had applied to two rather prestigious law firms for summer work, and was turned down by both of them.

"In my attempt to console him, to let him know that even when we are at our lowest there is hope, I realized that my words truly were empty without God. Right then and there, I came to the full understanding that I couldn't encourage him to keep on looking, to feel confident in himself unless I had a strong belief in something that could give me hope, and that something is God. After all these years, I have to admit that Mother was right, at least about God."

56

## Seventy-five Percenters

It is so sad that Jane's mother didn't understand her daughter's personality and even her own so that they could have been spared the pain they both suffered all those years. What's more, they had been robbed of many years of what should have been a blossoming relationship, spiritually and otherwise. But that's what happens when 75 percenters are pushed to the point of getting even. In doing so, they often hurt themselves just as badly as they hurt you.

Let's go back to the story of Denise and Bill from chapter 3. Denise, you remember, is a 25 percenter, while her brother Bill is a 75 percenter. In this particular case, we can readily see that unless parents are acquainted with personality types, whole families can be seriously damaged.

Mom and Dad were just as hard on Bill as they were on Denise, but he went on his way regardless.

Bill's parents forced him to go to college, so he went one year and quit. His mother had tried to direct his life just as she did Denise's, but his natural "I-can-do-it-myself" attitude made this extremely difficult. Bill and his mother were constantly at odds.

When Bill and Denise argued and their parents came down hard on them, Bill got angrier and Denise felt guiltier. As soon as he could, Bill got completely away from his family, adopting none of their values. Why should he? His parents were so busy making him mind that they rarely let him know how much they loved him.

However, when Denise's problems surfaced and the whole family entered counseling, many issues were brought to light and resolved. This family is so very fortunate. It is healing and the individual members are at last living happy, productive lives.

The stories of Denise, Bill, and Jane illustrate the extreme importance of thoroughly understanding each of our children on an individual basis. Unless we know who we are as parents, and unless we become intimately acquainted with our children, we can unintentionally do irreparable damage.

## Kids Who Follow, Kids Who Don't

Understanding each personality is the key to understanding how to handle each individual situation. Even though we are not more restrictive or more condoning or more permissive to either the 75 percenter or the 25 percenter, the better we know the personality, the better we are equipped to handle the whole child.

Very few kids have equal traits of both personalities, but they do exist. Such youngsters actually tend to lean one direction or the other, but not to the extent of the true 75 percenter and the true 25 percenter. Our daughter, Carey, is one of these middle-of-the-roaders. We were fortunate in having Carey first. If either of our two boys had been born first, then we would really have had problems.

If David had arrived first, I know he would not only be anti-Christian, but he wouldn't even be able to talk about it without going into a rage. Dale would probably be a Christian, but not a happy one who arrived at the decision of his own volition.

Now that you know whether you have a 25 percenter or a 75 percenter, you are armed with a tremendous amount of help to guide that child through life into spiritual adulthood. Spirituality will surely develop in the child whose parents have bothered to learn about his particular idiosyncrasies and have taken the time to show him that they love him unconditionally.

# 5

# A Generation of Angry Kids

*"A gentle answer turns away wrath, but a harsh word stirs up anger" (Proverbs 15:1).*

"What's for supper, Mom?" fourteen-year-old Tommy asked as he tossed his books and ball glove on the kitchen table.

"I haven't fixed any supper, Tom, but I have things all set to go for you and Daddy when he gets home," his mother answered. "I have to work at the office this evening."

"Oh, brother! I hate to cook! Can't you do this for us before you leave?"

"You'll do fine. Don't be so grouchy. What's wrong, anyway? You were angry the minute you walked through the door." Tommy's mother handed him the hamburger patties. "How was ball practice?"

"Fine!" Tommy snapped as he slammed the skillet down on the stove. "You wouldn't care even if it went terrible," he muttered, tossing the patties into the pan.

"Watch your tongue, young man! You don't need to get upset just because you have to fix two hamburgers. I don't want to hear anymore out of you!"

Tommy's dad walked in the back door. "I'm home! Hey, look who's fixing supper!"

"Yeah. Mom has to go to work."

"Looks like you have things pretty well underway, Son. I'll make a salad. What's new?"

"Nothing," Tommy replied sullenly.

"Hey, what's the trouble? You sound kind of moody."

"He's mad because he has to help with supper, and he must have had a bad ball practice," Tommy's mother answered for him; then kissed her husband on the cheek. "I'm going to work."

"I am not, Mom," Tommy angrily called to her as she left the room.

"Wait a minute, now; let's settle down. What *is* wrong with you, Tom? Why were you arguing with your mother when I came home?"

"I had a lousy ball practice, Dad. Nothing went right."

"Hold on, Tom. I don't want to hear you complain about baseball. If you can't take a little static from the coach, then I suggest you just drop out of the program. You're a good player and you know it, so just get in there and show them what you can do, and quit complaining."

"That's just it, Dad. At practice today I didn't do so . . . "

"I don't want to hear anymore about it! Either quit complaining or quit baseball. Which will it be?"

"I'll play ball," Tom conceded quietly.

"Now, what kind of dressing do you want on your salad?"

"Doesn't matter."

"Just leave the kitchen, Tom. This mood of yours is not something I want to put up with all evening. I'd like to know what in the world is wrong with you."

"But, Dad, I'm trying to tell you. At practice today . . . "

"No more talk about practice. Go to your room, and I'll call you when supper is ready."

Have you ever hit your thumb with a hammer and yelled? Have you ever had a tough day at work and couldn't wait to get home to discuss it? Have you ever felt angry and frustrated after watching the evening news and turned immediately to your spouse and voiced your opinion?

Chances are, you were able to answer yes to all these questions. All of us have felt anger and have felt the need to release that anger by yelling at or talking to someone.

Imagine how you would have felt if you were told you could not yell when you hit your thumb. And what if your spouse refused to listen to your tale of a bad day at work, or ignored you when you wanted to comment on the news telecast? Wouldn't that have been frustrating and made you angrier?

That's how Tommy felt when he tried to talk with his parents about ball practice—more frustrated and more angry. All he wanted to do was to get his anger out, but his parents were too busy to listen. It happens to all of us and we don't realize it. We get so involved in our own lives that we don't take the time to listen, really listen, to our children. Fortunately for Tommy and his parents, they resolved the problem the next morning.

Tommy's dad put his hand on the boy's shoulder and said, "Son, I'm sorry about last night. I should have listened to you instead of sending you to your room, but I'm not used to coming home and fixing supper, so I wasn't in the best of moods either. Let's hear about ball practice. Everyone is entitled to a bad one now and then. I know I had my share of them."

"And I was so busy getting ready for work that I didn't really take time to listen either, Tom," his mother added. "Don't give up on us, Son. The next time something goes wrong for you, we'll behave more like adults and listen to you." She smiled and gave his arm a squeeze.

## The Causes of Anger

Before further discussion on how to handle anger, let's find out what causes it. Any person will respond in an angry way if his emotional needs are not met as he expects they should be. Take a young child, for instance. When an infant is not fed the moment he wants to be fed, he becomes angry. If his diaper goes unchanged and he becomes uncomfortable, he gets angry.

As he gets a little older, he develops an emotional attachment to someone, usually his mother. It can be someone other than his mother, but regardless of who it is, if that person does not meet his needs, he becomes angry.

A perfect example of this is the time my wife, Pat, attended a weekend conference when our first son, David, was eighteen months old. Pat had never left David for that length of time before.

I anticipated no problems as Assistant Mom and had none. But two days later when Pat got home, David would have nothing to do with her. He was angry with his mother for leaving him—a perfectly normal reaction—and would not let her touch him for about six hours.

Pat was gone for only forty-eight hours, but look at kids today. Mothers or other adults leave them for long periods of time, and on a regular basis. And this is one significant reason why kids are so angry today—they are not given the loving attention they need to keep that anger from happening. They have a need for an emotional attachment, but nobody is there to fill that need.

The emotional needs of kids have to be met in certain behavioral ways by parents. Kids react more to *how* their parents behave toward them than what their parents say to them. They need positive eye contact, positive physical contact, focused attention, and loving discipline. I talked about these traits in my book *How to Really Love Your Child*, but I am going to briefly review them here.

All too often, parents use eye contact, that powerful means of communication, in a negative way. Knowing that a child is most attentive when we look him straight in the eye, we reserve eye contact for the times when we need to reprimand him. A young child will obey because of fear, but as he grows older, this fear gives way to anger and resentment. Consciously avoiding eye contact is just as damaging to a child. Indeed, it is more painful than corporal punishment. So let's couple eye contact with a smile and pleasant words, and take care of misbehavior in other ways.

Unfortunately, parents reserve physical contact only for times when kids need assistance, such as getting dressed and undressed or getting in and out of a car. This is sad because physical contact is one of the easiest ways to give children the unconditional love they so desperately need. All of us need positive physical contact with other human beings. Be honest now, don't you feel good when a friend puts an arm around you for an instant and tells you how glad he is to see you?

Focused attention takes work. It may often mean giving up something you had already planned, but it is a vital need in a child's life. Focused attention makes the child feel that he is the only one of his kind; he is special. All parents must take time to spend with each child individually. Recall how good you feel when you can spend time with your spouse, just the two of you, talking over the day, and you will understand the need a child has for that same kind of time.

Discipline is much more than applying the rod. It is training a child in mind and character, to enable him to become a self-controlled, constructive member of society. It involves guidance by example, verbal instruction, teaching, providing learning and fun experiences; in short, it encompasses every type of communication. It also involves punishment. Even though punishment is a negative and primitive factor of discipline, it must be used at times. However, the best form of discipline is guidance toward the correct thought and action, instead of punishment for wrong actions. Discipline is immeasurably easier when the child feels genuinely loved.

By giving our kids loving attention in these various ways, we are filling their emotional tanks. Far too many kids today are running around with empty emotional tanks, and far too many kids today are angry.

Lack of emotional nurturing causes depression, and depression causes anger. Many professionals who treat drug and alcohol addiction say that drugs and alcohol cause depression. This is true, but most kids who take drugs and alcohol are already depressed or on the way, due to not having their emotional needs met. Most people who deal with children neglect this fact.

Few people understand that a depressed child is an angry child. And the angrier he is, the likelier he is to become more depressed. It is a vicious cycle, and it can happen to any child regardless of his life experiences. It can happen to a rich kid, a poor kid, a kid with a lot of friends, a kid with few friends, a kid with many activities, a kid with few activities, and so on.

What's the answer? We must, first of all, give our children unconditional love and prevent some of their anger, and then teach them to handle their natural anger. We must allow them to let their anger out, instead of keeping it inside. Suppressed anger is a very dangerous thing.

## Passive-aggressive Behavior

Passive-aggressive behavior is suppressed anger that a child or an adult displays in a negative, albeit unconscious way. It is *normal* in only one time of life, and that is during early adolescence—ages thirteen through fifteen. Passive-aggressive behavior comes from an antiauthority attitude. It is anti-parent, anti-teacher, anti-Christian, anti-employer, anti-anything which represents authority. The purpose of passive-aggressive behavior is to upset authority—to make authority figures angry.

Some examples of passive-aggressive behavior are forgetfulness, dawdling, lying, stealing, and chronic lateness. Once you understand what passive-aggressive behavior is and are looking for it, you will find it everywhere.

Everyone exhibits some passive-aggressive behavior. For instance, if I don't watch myself, I tailgate when I drive. A child displays the same suppressed anger when he soils his pants after he has been toilet trained.

When Daniel was six years old, his mother had a baby boy. Now, Daniel had been the center of attention in his home for six years, so the arrival of this baby was a drastic change for him.

Every time he asked his mother to do something for him, she would be taking care of the baby. Whenever he wanted to crawl up on his dad's lap and read, the baby would be there. And whenever Daniel made any extra noise at all, his mother would tell him to be quiet because the baby was sleeping.

If Daniel wanted to hold or touch the baby, his parents would tell him that he couldn't. "You might hurt him," they would say. He didn't even get to push the baby stroller.

Poor Daniel. No matter where he turned, that baby was in his way. He wanted to complain, but everyone seemed too busy with the baby to listen.

Then one day, Daniel stood in the middle of the kitchen floor and soiled his pants. "Mom, come change me," he called. "I'm all dirty!"

Daniel was tired of being left out. He was angry and frustrated. He knew he couldn't yell and scream at his parents or the baby, so he chose an indirect way to get back at them. Subconsciously, the purpose of his action was to upset his parents. And it worked.

Passive-aggressive behavior is hard to see at first because it is so subtle. It almost invariably comes across in fine, upstanding people who initially seem very friendly. The reason they are easy to like in the first place is because they are pleasant. And the reason they appear so pleasant is because they have suppressed all their anger. We see only the pleasant people, but the anger is down there, waiting to come out.

An example of the subtlety of passive-aggressive behavior is easy to see in children, especially teenagers, and their problems with grades.

At the beginning of the school year, there is no reason for a student to be angry at the teacher or the school. This is especially the case when the student is attending a new school and has new teachers. He starts the school year doing very well. However, as the year progresses, the normal aggravations of life cause anger to gradually build up inside him.

He, like most passive-aggressive people, is very good at suppressing anger, but eventually the anger level gets so great that it starts coming out in passive-aggressive behavior. The grades start going down. The student unconsciously thinks, "I am so angry with you that I won't do the work." He doesn't even realize it's happening. Consciously, he wants to do as well as everyone else; unconsciously, he is releasing suppressed anger in a passive-aggressive way in order to upset authority—parents and/or teachers.

As I stated earlier, younger teens are naturally passive-aggressive to some extent. But if we can handle this phase of their lives correctly, they should be through the passive-aggressive stage by the time they are seventeen or eighteen.

Any thirteen-, fourteen-, or fifteen-year-old is unconsciously and sometimes consciously anti-almost anything—especially those who are 75 percenters. In fact, they are usually angry about something most of the time. What we must do is keep that anger coming out of their mouths instead of allowing them to keep it inside.

This is a very difficult thing for parents to do, because their natural inclination is to quiet their teenagers, suppress the kids' anger, and keep peace in the house. But sometimes I have to ask the parents I counsel, "Would you rather have a son yelling at you, or a son overdosed on drugs? Would you rather have a daughter harping and screaming, or have a pregnant daughter?"

I always tell parents to remove the pressure from their younger teens by allowing these kids to verbalize their anger. In this way, *they* learn to maturely control their tempers. In this way, *we* train our children as Proverbs says we should.

Suppressing anger is something like depressing an inflated balloon with a bulge in it; if you push the bulge in, it is going to come out somewhere else. So, if we try to keep our children from expressing their anger, it will only pop out in some other area of their lives—in negative, usually passive-aggressive behavior.

Bear in mind that you can't totally prevent passive-aggressive behavior, even though you allow your teen to verbalize. You need a safety valve for passive-aggressive attitudes to come out in a harmless way. You see, passive-aggressive behavior is primarily unconscious, and the unconscious mind is amoral. It really doesn't care whether the thought is right or wrong; it just has to get rid of anger.

In passive-aggressive behavior, a teenager gets rid of anger by making his parents upset. So whatever upsets the parents most is what the kid is going to go for—the jugular! What would upset Christian parents most? Where is the primary interest in most Christian homes? It is spirituality, of course. So where is the kid's passive-aggressive behavior going to be targeted? Against spirituality, of course.

In non-Christian homes, on the other hand, and in some Christian homes as well, generally the emphasis is on grades, so most passive-aggressive behavior starts out antiacademics, anti-learning. Either area can be very destructive in the long run. But what can we do to prevent such a result?

First, we can avoid making big issues out of spiritual things and academics, especially during these years of adolescence. Now, if your teen comes to you and wants to talk, that's great. You are in a different situation. When the teen initiates the conversation, that means you are not the one doing the preaching or displaying any negative or authoritarian attitudes. Overemphasizing anything during these years is just handing the kid ammunition and saying, "Hey, here's how you can hurt me and yourself. Have at it."

Now, can you think of a harmless passive-aggressive behavior? (Keep in mind that passive-aggressive behavior is an unconscious act by a person doing the opposite of what you want him to do.) What about a messy room? That's a very normal passive-aggressive behavior in almost any teen, because parents are always demanding, "Clean up your room!"

If your daughter's room is messy, it's a good place for you as a parent to put emphasis because it's a passive-aggressive behavior which will not hurt anybody. Why?

Because you want to make an issue only out of something that is unimportant and will not hurt the child. So go ahead and put emphasis on cleaning up that room. She'll eventually outgrow that anti-everything, passive-aggressive attitude and put her room in order again. But how much better for her to exhibit passive-aggressive behavior by keeping a messy room, instead of going against spirituality or making low grades.

In the young child and the young teenager, up to about age sixteen or seventeen, passive-aggressive behavior can be changed. That is, we can teach our children to express their anger positively, so that passive-aggressive behavior will not develop any more than it normally does in that stage of life.

However, once the teen reaches the ages of sixteen to eighteen, passive-aggressive behavior can solidify. At that point, it can be very difficult, almost impossible, to change. This is why it is so critical to take care of these things as early in childrearing as possible. Not only should we be careful not to make our children passive-aggressive in spiritual matters, but in all other areas as well, because passive-aggressiveness permeates the whole being.

## When Passive-aggressive Kids Grow Up

Passive-aggressive behavior is one of the primary forces operating in the world—internationally, nationally, locally, up and down your street. For example, many telling illustrations of adult passive-aggressive behavior can be found in employer-employee relationships.

An employer does not detect passive-aggressive behavior when he is conducting an interview with a prospective employee. Indeed, it can take months before a new employee begins exhibiting it. Just like the child starting a new school with a new teacher, the employee starts his new job with a positive attitude. Everything goes along great—for a while.

Then things start going wrong. The employee gets a little irritated here, a little angry there, and the anger gradually increases to the point where passive-aggressive behavior starts exhibiting itself in antiauthority gestures. His job proficiency begins to decrease, and the desirability to have him as an employee becomes less and less. Finally, the employee causes so much conflict that he has to be fired.

The main difference between passive-aggressive behavior in children and similar behavior in adults is that it is largely unconscious in children, and more conscious in adults. It usually only starts unconsciously in adults, and gradually develops into a conscious action.

A short time ago, a businessman friend of mine decided to hire an office manager.

"You know, Ross," he said to me, "I thought this would be a perfect arrangement. I could work in the field more, and he could handle questions from clients, some public relations work, collections, etc. In short, Everett seemed like the answer to my problems.

"And he was—for a time. We had agreed on a small salary until he learned the job, and then he would receive increases based on his productivity.

"All seemed to be going quite well until one of my field men had to stay in the office for a few days to do some work. My secretary was unable to do the typing needed to complete his work, because she was filling in for Everett, who for some unknown reason had taken three days off."

"Had he asked for the time off?" I asked my friend.

"No, he just took it. I had talked with him a few weeks earlier, and learned that he had real difficulties getting along with his father, who had just recently passed away. He stated at the time that he might need a few days off to help his mother settle legal matters incurred by his father's death, but he never asked for any particular days.

"At any rate, I considered the circumstances, and let the matter drop. A few weeks later, my secretary told me that Everett was missing work regularly. I talked with him about it, and he said that he had taken a part-time job because I wasn't paying him enough. He had bought a car, and he and his wife were talking about moving to a higher rent area. He said he had understood that I would be giving him a raise, but I hadn't come through.

"I reminded him of our original agreement, and he became very angry with me, accusing me of not caring about him or his family.

"Shortly after this confrontation, I had occasion to work in the office for a few days. It afforded me ample opportunity to see my office manager in action. He did very little. He ignored most of the collection matters, turning them over to the secretary. He made no attempts at pursuing possible clients. In short, he was almost nonproductive.

"I tried to talk with him, but he became hostile, so I threatened to cut his wages if he didn't start to work on some of our accounts.

"This threat alarmed him, so for about six months, he made weak attempts at fulfilling his job. I even gave him a raise in pay, hoping this would be an incentive, but still, every time I worked in the field, he found excuses to leave the office. His excuse for being gone so much was that he was interviewing possible new clients, but none ever materialized.

"He was such a burden that I finally fired him. To this day, he blames me for all the problems we had. He contends that he did everything he was supposed to do. He says that he worked like a dog, and I treated him horribly."

When I learned that Everett had never gotten along with his father, I was not surprised at the way the interaction between him and my friend developed.

Everett had set up the situation so that he would have an excuse to be angry with his boss. Passive-aggressive behavior transfers directly from the parent to the spouse and then to the employer. Unconsciously and consciously, Everett was doing all that he could to make my friend angry, all the while rationalizing that he was right. The more passive-aggressive a person is, the more he can rationalize. I really could sympathize with my friend. I have worked with passive-aggressive adults, and it is difficult. They rationalize most actions they take.

Another example of working with a passive-aggressive person is when I hired a young woman to work in our clinic. At first, everything went very well. She was a pleasant and kind person and a good secretary.

Then, just like a typical passive-aggressive individual, she became less and less accountable as the months went on. She began to arrive at work late, until finally her tardiness became just plain flagrant. Some days she didn't show up for work at all. And her lunch hour nearly always extended beyond the allotted time.

Since I hate to fire people, I put up with her actions for a long time. Then I began to see her attitude show up in her work. She began to leave work for the other secretaries in the office to complete, which caused them to complain, and rightfully so.

71

The irony of the situation was that because she was such a pleasant person, those who did not have to work directly with her really liked her. However, those who had to do the work which she left undone resented her. So she created a tremendous amount of turmoil for the entire office.

Anyway, one Friday at noon (Friday is absolutely the busiest day of the week for us), she quit her job and walked out. There was no reason for her action; nothing unusual had gone wrong in the office; she simply quit, leaving the other secretaries in a difficult situation.

The next day she phoned me to apologize for her action, then asked for her job back. I just couldn't bring myself to tell her no, so I told her to come back to work on Monday. She had, as typical passive-aggressive people will do, made promises of doing better.

When I hung up the phone, I started thinking about the whole situation and realized that things were not going to get better. In fact, I knew that in less than a week, things would be even worse than they were before. So I called her back and told her not to return. I felt terrible doing it, but I knew I had to do it. I can't tell you the difference it has made in our office.

Once more, I want to emphasize that everyone is passive-aggressive to some extent. It shows up in the driving habits of some people; others display it by constantly showing up late for meetings; the list is endless. But it is only when passive-aggressive behavior totally takes over a person's life that it is a pathological personality disorder.

Passive-aggressive adults will be the end result of today's kids if we don't start helping them deal with their anger now.

## Helping a Child Deal with Anger

The younger a child is, the more immaturely he will express his anger. As he matures, he should begin to learn to express his

72

anger in a more positive way. This is where we, as parents, must have patience.

I realize that many times parents are so tired that they simply want to tell their child to "Be quiet!" but that is absolutely the worst thing to do. It only succeeds in cramming his anger deep inside him. I would like to discuss ways to help children and teenagers express their anger in a positive way—a way that will clear the air much better than "Be quiet!"

In order to help parents deal with the complexities of resolving anger, I have created an Anger Ladder. There are fifteen rungs on the ladder, each one higher representing a progressively better way of expressing anger:

1. Pleasant behavior
2. Seeking resolution
3. Focusing anger on source only
4. Holding to the primary complaint
5. Thinking logically and constructively
6. Unpleasant and loud behavior
7. Cursing
8. Displacing anger to sources other than the original
9. Expressing unrelated complaints
10. Throwing objects
11. Destroying property
12. Verbal abuse
13. Emotionally destructive behavior
14. Physical abuse
15. Passive-aggressive behavior

And now we need to put this ladder to good use. As we discussed earlier, passive-aggressive behavior is the worst way to express anger. Going out of control behaviorally to the point of property destruction or violence toward another person sounds bad, but still is better than passive-aggressive behavior. Only slightly, but better because it is easier to deal with and prevent than passive-aggressive behavior.

A still slightly better way of expressing anger is to be in a fit of rage. This may involve screaming, cursing, yelling, name-calling—all directed not only at the source of the anger, but to anyone else who happens to be in the vicinity. As poor as this expression of anger seems to be, it too is far better than passive-aggressive behavior.

Climbing up the ladder, we come to verbal release of anger, aimed at anyone within hearing distance. As poor as this may sound, it also is an improvement over those mentioned thus far.

Getting near the top of the ladder, we find a good way of expressing anger in Rung #3, and that is focusing it only on the source. This may involve some yelling and screaming, but at least it is confined to the provoker of the anger.

The top of the ladder is the best of all ways to resolve anger, and that is pleasant and rational expression toward the person with whom you are angry. It is hoped that the person with whom you are having the problem will respond in an equally mature way, so that both parties can rationally and logically examine the issue, discuss it, and agree what to do about it. Few people come to this point of maturity, but if your teen can occasionally see you handle your anger in this manner, he has a good background for reaching such a point himself.

Expect your teenager to become angry at times, and encourage him to express it verbally. Then, determine where he is on the Anger Ladder, and work with him from there. Find a time after you both have calmed down to praise your teen in the areas where he expressed his anger correctly; then ask him to correct the aspect you think needs changing.

Let me clarify one point that might possibly be confusing. I am speaking of *verbal* expressions of anger, not behavioral expressions of anger. I am not encouraging permissiveness in behavior; I am encouraging verbal expressions of anger which can finally be developed into positive methods of resolving anger.

# A Generation of Angry Kids

An example of helping a teen deal with anger happened to a friend of ours whose teenager came home from school with a very low grade on a math test.

Jerry, a bright, outgoing, high-school junior, walked into the house, threw his books on the front hall table, and stomped into the kitchen. Finding nothing in the refrigerator to please him, he slammed the door shut.

"Sure looks like you could keep something around here to eat, Mom," he growled, and headed toward his room, stumbling over his little brother's blocks. He immediately yelled, "Bobby, get out here and pick up these toys! You're more trouble than you're worth! I could've broken my ankle!"

"OK, Jerry, that's about enough," said his mother. "I know you're angry about something, but I doubt that it's the lack of food in the refrigerator or Bobby's toys. I do appreciate the fact that you're getting your anger out, but let's try to settle down somewhat and get to the bottom of this." She remained calm, and placed her hand on Jerry's shoulder. "Did something go wrong at school today?"

Jerry brought his books from the hall table, and handed his mother the test paper. "Not unless you call a D on an important math test something wrong," he answered her sarcastically.

"Do you want to talk about it now, or wait a little while?"

"I don't understand this low grade, Mom." Jerry's voice softened. "These problems look right to me. I don't know any other way to solve them."

"What do you think about talking to your teacher about this tomorrow, and maybe he can tell you why he marked them wrong?"

"He won't listen. He's one of those people who know everything."

"Maybe if you talk with him, Jerry, you'll find that he's not such a bad person. Teachers appreciate the pupil who is interested in learning."

Jerry finally decided to talk with his teacher. The next evening he was in a good mood. "Guess what, Mom! You were right. My math teacher had made an error in grading my paper, and I got a B on the test."

Jerry's mother was wise in letting him verbalize his frustration, and then in helping him get to the real reason for the anger.

It is so important to understand that whether we are dealing with teenagers, employees, unions, or government, anger is inevitable. It can result from any human interaction. We must also realize that if anger is not dealt with, it will become more and more difficult to control—even explosive. The more it builds up, the more destructive it can become.

Therefore, we must help our teens "nip it in the bud" if the anger is based on a misunderstanding or, if the anger is justified, verbally vent it in a slow, positive way so that it can be resolved.

This method of anger resolution does not come naturally to anyone. We, as parents, must patiently train our teens to manage their anger in a mature way. We must guide them toward positive verbalization of their anger, not allowing behavioral outbursts. We must be careful that our teens' anger does not stay inside, creating passive-aggressive adults.

An angry adult cannot be a productive person. He cannot accept authority of any kind, including spiritual authority. "For man's anger does not bring about the righteous life that God desires" (James 1:20).

# 6

# Christian Discipline

*"As a father has compassion on his children, so the Lord has compassion on those who fear Him" (Psalm 103:13).*

I get very upset when I read child-rearing books written by prominent Christian leaders who advocate hitting, yelling, and pinching as ways to keep children under control. These writers lightly pass over the basic need of the child, which is a need for unconditional love and acceptance.

In this chapter, you are not going to read that beating the child with the rod and pinching him are sound child-rearing practices. You are not going to be told that he is a depraved and evil being who needs his will broken. (I just recently read that description written by an "expert.") By the same token, neither are you going to read that total permissiveness is the answer to child-rearing woes.

If you are handling your child in any of these ways, and you firmly believe that you are doing the right thing, then you might be turned off by what you are about to read. But please don't lay this book down. Hear me out. If you are turned off because this is not what you are used to hearing, then both you and your child are going to benefit greatly. You are going to learn that you can lovingly discipline your child, and rest in the assurance that he will become an acceptable human being at the same time.

The last thing you want to have to do is use harsh disciplinarian measures on your child. I know that if you follow my suggestions, and take the few extra minutes required to get to the reasons for misbehavior, much harsh action can be avoided. The misbehavior itself will oftentimes be avoided if you have established a relationship of unconditional love with your child.

It takes time and patience, but who is more important than your child? No talent at all is involved in telling your child to shut up. And anybody can hit a child when he opens his mouth in disagreement. Unfortunately for parents and children alike, too many child-rearing experts are advocating that very thing. This is discouraging, because it results in a child never getting through the normal passive-aggressive stage. He remains passive-aggressive on into adulthood.

### Loving, Christlike Discipline

I have discussed various ways of conveying love to children, such as eye contact, focused attention, and physical contact. Now I am going to discuss more fully the idea of loving discipline. To administer loving discipline is to train the child in the way he should go. It does not mean forcing the child to go the way you want him to go.

Let's go back a step. Even before you can train your child in the way he should go, he must have and feel from you unconditional love. A child who feels unloved is an angry child, and an angry child will not respond to *any* kind of discipline in a positive way.

Anytime you are unjustly harsh to your children, you are violating Ephesians 6:4, which reads: "Fathers, do not provoke your children to anger; but bring them up in the discipline and instruction of the Lord" (NASB).

Originally, the word *discipline* meant "an instruction imparted

78

to disciples." Today, a more negative meaning of the word is favored. Most Christian child-rearing "experts" define *discipline* as "control." They place minimal emphasis on first loving your child, and then they launch into instructions on how to control your child. This is unfortunate, because too much enforced control only serves to anger kids.

As I stated earlier, suppressed anger is very damaging to children. It can create all kinds of problems as they enter their teen years. Giving unconditional love and attempting to understand the reason or reasons for children's misbehavior are the best solutions for solving their problems.

If you can keep the original meaning of *discipline* in mind as you work with your children, it will be of great help to you. The first thing most of us think of when we hear the word *disciple* (discipline being an instruction imparted to disciples) is Christ's disciples. The deepest wish of these twelve men was to be exactly like Christ.

How do you think Christ convinced these men that they should follow Him? Do you think that they believed in Him just because He told them to? Of course not. The disciples followed Christ because of their love for Him and His love for them. "We love because He first loved us" (1 John 4:19).

They would never have made such radical changes in their lives if they had not loved Him and felt His love in return. The love of God through Christ was given to the disciples, and they became eager to follow His teachings and spread His Word.

The beautiful example of Christ and His disciples clearly shows us that love and admiration are powerful motives for people to adopt another's values. This example can be followed by parents as they train their children in the way they should go.

Mutual love is the very best way to get children to adopt your values. Once this foundation has been established, not only will your children adopt your general lifestyle, but you will have achieved your primary goal for them—they will want to adopt your spiritual values.

Discipline, then, as I have just defined it, is *training* the child. Physical punishment is only one part of discipline and if the child has had his emotional needs met, a very small part.

## The Misuse of Corporal Punishment

Anyone can physically strike a child in a moment of anger, but it takes time and patience to train him. I am not saying that physical punishment should never be used; I am suggesting that loving guidance based on firmly preestablished rules will benefit the entire family structure much more.

A problem that frequently arises is that the punishment far outweighs the crime. I remember talking with a young mother whose four-year-old daughter took two or three board games from the game closet and mixed them all together.

"I just had a fit, Dr. Campbell," the mother exclaimed. "I yelled at her, and then demanded that she separate all those pieces and put them back in the proper boxes. It was a task for an adult, but I made her stick with it. It took almost two hours of tears and yelling, but she got it done."

"How do you think you should have handled the situation?" I asked her.

"I realize now that I should have worked with her. She is entirely too young to have been given such a monumental task and carry it through. What makes me feel so badly is that I spanked her the minute I saw the mess. Parents surely can be cruel."

This mother is so right. Parents can be cruel. They don't set out to be cruel; it just happens. As I read many of the child-rearing books written today, I can readily understand why. Corporal punishment is the main theme.

It makes me sad to see people emphasize the four verses from Proverbs which deal with using the rod (13:24; 23:13-14;

80

29:15), and then see them virtually ignore Scripture which deals with the child's most basic need—love.

Hundreds of verses in the Bible instruct us to be understanding, compassionate, sensitive, nurturing, and forgiving. Our children are very deserving, and have every right to these expressions of love.

One crucial point overlooked by so-called child-rearing experts is the fact that corporal punishment can be physically damaging to the child. When the use of the rod is needed, it must be done with extreme caution.

An unfortunate consequence of corporal punishment is that it alleviates guilt. Too much guilt can be damaging to a child, but he must learn to feel some guilt in order to develop a conscience.

A spanking will clear the air; that is certain. The child feels no guilt because he has paid for his wrongdoing by being spanked. The parent has released his anger by spanking the child, so it would appear that everything is under control. However, the lesson learned by the child is not that his misbehavior was wrong, only that he shouldn't get caught at it the next time.

What you really want for your child is for him to develop a normal, healthy conscience. This will help him control future actions. Feeling guilty once in a while will aid in this development. So, the next time your child misbehaves, try letting him "sit one out." Give him time to think about his actions and their consequences. In other words, give him time to feel some good, honest guilt for his wrongdoing.

Another consequence of corporal punishment is aggressor identification. This also is a way of escaping guilt. The child sides with the parent, and begins to agree that aggressive and abusive actions are right. The sad thing about this result is that the child takes this attitude into his adult life, and treats his children and others the same way.

## Kids Who Follow, Kids Who Don't

My strong advice is to stand up against those who are saying that the primary way to discipline a child is to physically punish him. Some of these "experts" don't even have children of their own. Let us adopt the attitude of Christ which He presented daily to His disciples; let us unconditionally love our children so that they will want to adopt our ways and values.

I don't want to mislead you and let you think that if you love your child unconditionally, he will never misbehave. I'm a parent too, and I know that simply is not true! I have learned though that dealing with misbehavior is made easier if you have a firm, love-based relationship with your child.

When a child misbehaves, the first thing we should ask ourselves is, "Why did this child take this action?" or "Does he have a need that I am not meeting or have not met?" Our first thought should *not* be a negative one, such as, "What can I do to correct this kid's behavior?"

Remember the story of Daniel in chapter 5? Daniel misbehaved by soiling his pants because he felt unloved. Let's imagine two possible reactions from his parents to this event. If his parents respond to his misbehavior by spanking him and sending him to his room, they will not solve his problem. They will not fulfill his needs. Therefore, the problem will probably reoccur.

Daniel's parents need to fill his emotional tank. They need to make him feel loved too. In doing so, they will take away the reason for the misbehavior, thus eliminating future misbehavior of this kind.

Teachers sometimes mishandle their students' negative actions. Not long ago, I was counseling Molly, who told me of a very painful experience she had with her teacher.

Molly had been late for school three mornings in one week. On the third morning, her teacher punished her tardiness by making her crawl to her desk. Then he struck her hands with a ruler. This was an extreme action, and one which proved painfully embarrassing for Molly.

# Christian Discipline

Had the teacher bothered to check, he would have found that the reason she had been late was because the street on her usual route to school had been closed. He would also have discovered that both of her parents worked, and she was left alone each morning to get herself ready for school. If only Molly had been able to give her reasons before such stern punishment was administered, she might not have needed counseling. If only the teacher had taken just a few minutes with her, he could have been her trusted friend instead of just a strict teacher for whom she had no respect.

I am not advocating that you condone misbehavior. Try instead to arrive at the reason for the misbehavior. Once that is accomplished, the misbehavior will be clearly understood and not likely repeated.

Neither am I telling you to never spank your child. I am simply suggesting that you put it on the very bottom of your list of productive and fair ways to deal with misbehavior—a last resort.

I am reminded of a little girl who lived in my neighborhood when I was a child. She had a pet kitten which she treated as though it were human. We used to tease her about that cat, and tried to take it away from her, but she guarded it with her life.

One day, she tied a ribbon about its neck and turned it loose. The ribbon got caught in the shrubs, and strangled the kitten.

When her father found out about it, he spanked her and yelled at her in full view of us kids. In looking back at that situation, I realize now that she needed some loving forgiveness for her actions. She was not a mean little girl. She would never have harmed that kitten on purpose.

She needed to talk with her father in the privacy of their home, and tell him how sorry she was and how bad she felt. She needed her father's forgiveness. After all, our Father in heaven forgives us when we confess doing wrong; shouldn't we do the same for our children?

Children need to feel forgiven when they are genuinely sorry for their actions. This helps them handle their guilt. I stated earlier that some guilt is necessary in order for the development of a conscience, but too much guilt can be very damaging. Allowing children to feel forgiven will save them untold serious problems of handling guilt in their adult lives.

You are making a grave mistake if you think that punishment in itself will solve anything. Punishment without unconditional love will result in a poor relationship between you and your child. And, if it is allowed to develop, by the time your child is an adult, he will not want to adopt any of your values. He will purposely go in exactly the opposite direction.

## Lifestyle Parenting

Young children have a need to admire their parents. These are the years, up to about age thirteen, that much positive groundwork can be laid for a solid relationship between you and your child. Focused attention during these years is very healthy for the child because it tells him that he is indeed very special. This is the time to teach and train the child spiritual values, and to emphasize them.

As he matures, he will begin to question much of what his parents stand for. He may even think they are deficient in some areas of their lives. Still, he has the strong need, though it is sometimes unconscious, to be able to love and admire them. So, it is obvious that a good, self-disciplined example set by you as parents will greatly influence the child in a positive way.

The old maxim, "Do as I say, not as I do" simply will not work with children. A few years ago, a study was conducted on the surge of undisciplined behavior of teenagers in Sweden. Researchers found that delinquents did not necessarily come from undisciplined, troubled homes. A higher percentage of troubled teens came from homes where the parents did not

84

Christian Discipline

practice the kind of lifestyles that they demanded of their children. The well-behaved, well-adjusted teen was found to come from the home of the parents who lived the lifestyle they expected of their children.

Always keep in mind, as you set examples for your children, that you are human and occasionally humans tire. During the child-rearing years, parents can deplete their emotional and physical strength. I especially suggest to parents of teens that they first make sure that their own physical well-being is tended to. By the time children become teens, parents are a little quicker to anger, a little less understanding, and a little more likely to handle their teens' anger with anger. I caution you not to fall into this trap. Keep up your own health so that you will be able to maintain self-control.

Your teen is going to challenge and/or break some of the rules that you set for him. Since you know this is going to happen, the thing to do in the beginning is to make the rules quite strict and restrictive. Then, as your teen matures and demonstrates that he can be trusted to behave as the situation demands, his privileges will gradually increase, and parental control will gradually lessen.

In gradually removing restrictions and granting privileges, you are teaching your teen to become a responsible, trustworthy, independent adult by the age of eighteen. This is not easy. It takes real courage to say no to your teen when other parents are allowing their teens to do things that you know are detrimental to their well-being.

Let me assure you of one absolute fact. Your teen, whether he realizes it consciously or not, wants your guidance and control. I have heard many young people say that their parents don't love them because their mothers and fathers are not strict or firm with them.

Teens must experience consequences for their behavior. They must experience positive consequences for positive, responsible behavior, and negative consequences for inappropriate, irresponsible behavior. These consequences must be consistent and fair, not based on how the parent is feeling at the time. Again, parental self-control is of the utmost importance.

It is good to keep in touch with other parents. In doing so, all of you can share valuable information and concerns about your children. You can work together in providing direction and discipline for them.

If you clearly state to your teenager that you are working to help him become a responsible, independent person, he can then feel you are *for* him, not *against* him. Such a positive attitude will greatly improve your relationship.

## The Four Types of Discipline

There are basically four types of discipline. The first is an *authoritarian* approach. The child is kept totally under control by his parents. He is offered no love, eye contact, physical contact, or focused attention.

The second type of discipline is the *authoritative* method. This method—based on unconditional love—offers the child a lot of direction, and correction when needed. He also receives emotional nurturing.

*Permissiveness* is the third disciplining method. It offers the child love, attention, and support, but absolutely no direction. The parent who uses this method just goes along with whatever the child decides, never correcting him or offering him overarching guidance.

The fourth method of dealing with a child is not to deal with him at all—*neglect.*

Recently, a study was conducted on four groups of young adults, each of which had received one of the four types of discipline. The results of the study were compared with the following:

1. Identification with the parents and their value system
2. Following parents' religious beliefs
3. Identification with counterculture movements (anti-authority attitudes)

The study revealed that the children who were raised under the *authoritative* method (where they not only received guidance, correction, and direction, but unconditional love) turned out the best. They not only *identified* with their parents' value system, but they made it through the antiauthority years and *adopted* the religious beliefs of Dad and Mom.

The kids who turned out to be the most unsettled adults were raised in an *authoritarian* manner. This is the way most children in Christian homes are raised and, not surprisingly, most reject Christ. The next to the worst way of raising children is pure *neglect*, and the second best way of raising children is *permissiveness*.

Aren't these findings amazing? Permissiveness, which is what Christian parents are strongly warned against, is superior to authoritarianism, which most Christian parents use. Even more annoying is the fact that the authoritarian method is worse than neglecting the child.

This study affirms my line of thinking: the authoritative way of raising children is the most successful. Children who are lovingly disciplined and guided to adulthood will eventually not only adopt, but *want* to adopt their parents' spiritual values.

## A Test of Your Discipline Methods

The following situations, which happen to all of us in our daily dealings with our children, can be answered with: (a) Try to find out why, and then deal with the problem accordingly; (b) Verbally punish him, and send him to his room; (c) Immediately administer corporal punishment, and discuss the problem later.

## Kids Who Follow, Kids Who Don't

1. When my child lies, I ____.
2. When my child makes low grades in school, I ____.
3. When my child refuses to eat his meals, I ____.
4. When my child is argumentative with me and I've had a rough day at the office, I ____.
5. When my child fights, I ____.
6. If my child ever stole anything, I would ____.
7. If my teenager puts a dent in the car, I will ____.
8. When my teenager comes in after curfew, I ____.
9. If my teenager begins to use drugs, I will ____.
10. If my teenager cheats on tests at school, I will ____.

Honestly check your answers to these random questions in the privacy of your home. If you find that your answers are predominantly "b" and "c", then you have probably bought into the authoritarian approach to discipline.

Reevaluate your child-rearing methods. Ask yourself if you are giving your child the loving attention and positive direction that he needs. It is critical for the all-around development of your child that he be made aware on a daily basis of your love for him.

# 7

# Children Want to Learn

*"Train up a child in the way he should go, and when he is old he will not turn from it"* (Proverbs 22:6).

A red sports car pulled up in front of the church and stopped. Two well-dressed little girls, about ages eight and ten, hopped out of the car. "You two wait right here on the church steps after Sunday School. Daddy and I will be back to get you at 11 o'clock."

"All right, Mommy. See you later." The children bounced up the steps and into the building while their parents sped away. They didn't want to be late for their tennis game.

"Ah, two whole hours just for us," the husband said, smiling at his wife. "We can get in about an hour of tennis, and then have breakfast before we have to pick up the girls. Sounds good, eh?"

"Sure does, Honey. We need this time each week. It's good for both of us."

Does this scenario sound familiar? Do you see your neighbor here or one of your friends? Or do you possibly see yourself? Churches throughout the nation are experiencing the problem of absentee parents.

Children learn by parental example. What are these girls

learning? Sadly, they are learning that just as soon as they are as old as Mommy and Daddy, they too can play tennis on Sunday mornings.

These parents have probably *told* their children that they are Christians, but they are not *living* their spiritual statements. Children are most apt to respond to the value system that their parents *live*, and less likely to respond to what is *told* to them. Parents are very mistaken if they think they can fool their children.

## Teaching Tots to Trust

Children are born ready to learn. In the early months of their lives, they have a built-in survival system. They let out a lusty yell to make their needs known.

A popular current theory on child-rearing advises parents not to pick up a baby every time he cries, because soon he will become spoiled. Actually, just the opposite happens. Babies who have been soothed at their every cry during their early months seem to develop into stronger, more self-confident children than babies who have been left to "cry it out."

When their needs are met during these first months, infants are learning that someone loves them. I don't know where the idea of ignoring a crying baby got started, but I disagree with it. By meeting his needs, you are establishing a mutual trust between you and your child.

As he develops from infancy into the toddler years, this same trust will be increased as you interact with him. A good method of teaching your toddler that you trust him is allowing him to do simple chores.

As you are putting away the pots and pans, allow him to put one away. I realize that a two-year-old is not going to properly complete this task on the first try, but that's all right. The whole point is to teach him. Even though he places a pan on the wrong shelf in an upside-down position, compliment him. Let him know that you are very pleased about what he did.

"Thank you, Tony. That looks so nice. I like having you help me put things away." Now Tony is learning two things. He is learning that you trust him, and he is developing self-esteem.

As you go through the toddler stage with your child, and you are trying to develop mutual trust, don't put too many temptations before him. I might suggest that you decorate your home as simply as possible. This serves two purposes. It makes housekeeping chores lighter, and it keeps you from constantly having to stop your child from picking up a favorite vase or knickknack.

The result of having too many temptations sitting around the house is that you will find yourself yelling constantly because you will not always have your hands free to retrieve that cherished heirloom. Raising your voice to your child has its place, but save it for that place.

On a recent trip to the bookstore, I picked up a book on child-rearing written by a Christian author. As I thumbed through the pages, I couldn't believe what I was reading. The author was telling his readers that it is not only permissible, but actually good, for infants from four or five months to be reprimanded by loud verbal instruction.

As I said, raising your voice is sometimes necessary, but not in the nursery of a six-month-old infant! An example of the need to raise your voice is if your small child darts away from you into a heavily traveled street. Then you would have to yell at him to possibly save his life. However, if you had been raising your voice at him since he was an infant, he quite probably wouldn't have paid any attention to you, and would have continued on his way.

This same author went on to tell parents that incorrect disciplinary actions will do no harm to their children. He explained that children are flexible and tough and forget quickly. Is it any wonder that we have so many hurting children

91

today, with child-rearing books like that on the market?

Swiss scientist Jean Piaget theorized that the development of learning in children is divided into four stages. The age-range of these stages is from birth to two years, from two to seven years, from seven to eleven years, and from eleven years on.

Two- to seven-year-olds believe exactly what their parents tell them. Indeed, until he gradually develops the ability to reason and question, a child takes most everything his parents say quite literally. Let me give you this amusing, but true example.

Three-year-old Adam sat quietly in the backseat of the car with his eight-year-old sister, Leeann. They were on their way home from the zoo.

"I'm really tired, Mom," Leeann announced, "and I have a headache."

"I do too," interrupted Adam. "Right here on my knuckle," he continued, pointing to the top of his head.

"Oh, Adam, your knuckle is on your hand, not on your head," Leeann replied with childish impatience. "Mom, would you please tell Adam that he can't get a headache in his knuckle?"

"I can too, Leeann!" Adam insisted. "Mommy always pats me on the head, and calls me a little knucklehead!"

You can readily see by the way Adam reacted to being lovingly called "Mommy's little knucklehead" that it would be very easy to put negative thoughts into the minds of our children because they are so trusting and believing.

I am reminded of an incident that happened to a friend when he was a child. His Sunday School teacher told the class how very pleased she was to be able to teach them about Jesus. "You know," she continued, "Jesus said, 'Suffer the little children to come unto Me.' "

"You know what happened when she read that verse to me, Ross? I began to fear going to Sunday School because I thought I would be nailed to a cross and suffer as Jesus did."

## Children Want to Learn

My friend was like Adam. He believed exactly what was said to him. The point I want to make here is that these trusting young minds are perfect for laying a strong foundation of spiritual values. These are the years when you are in the position to help your child expand emotionally, psychologically, and physically, as well as spiritually. It is absolutely crucial that you begin during these early years to develop your child as a whole person. Only the whole person can develop into a happy, responsible adult who will carry your spiritual values with him.

Our children are very sensitive to the responses they receive from us. They know when we are telling them something just to keep them quiet; they sense that we're not really interested in them at that moment.

A busy, single mother of three sons told me of an incident which occurred in her home, and it points out just how well our children know us.

She works during the week, so Saturday mornings are reserved especially for the boys. They plan shopping trips or whatever else pleases them for these special hours.

On a particularly busy Saturday when she was helping them dress for a trip to the mall, the oldest asked for assistance in tying his shoes.

"Sit here on this chair and I'll help you," she rather absent-mindedly stated. He quickly complied, and as he hopped down with his shoes neatly tied, the second one asked the same favor, and then the third.

Realizing that their mother wasn't totally listening to them or paying any attention to them, the oldest boy untied his shoes and got back up on the chair. "Will you tie my shoes, Mom?" he asked again. The second boy caught on, and untied his shoes, giggling quietly.

"Sure," the mother said, and began round two of tying shoes. Before the third one could get up on the chair, the mother saw what was going on.

Given the pressures of daily life for this young mother of three, it is understandable that this amusing incident happened, and probably many others which were at times unfair for the boys. But she has developed a stable, quality family unit, and so the significance of the negative incidents is minor.

As your child begins to mature to the point of not needing parental help with basic daily tasks, such as dressing or bathing, it is very easy for you to fill this time slot with other jobs. The danger here is that soon you will find yourself spending less and less time with your child. Finding time in today's hectic world is difficult, sometimes seemingly impossible, but you must do it. You must steal away a little time each day for your child, even if it means giving up something that you wanted just for yourself.

## The Power of Family Togetherness

Today, more than any other time in history, children are being influenced by forces outside the family. Many times children would rather spend time with the television than with you. Given what is offered on television, you have all the more reason to make the time to spend with your child.

Children just naturally want to learn. If you don't take the time or think you don't have the time to teach them, they will learn from someone else. They can be easily influenced by negative experiences outside the home. Research shows that even children as young as fifth-graders are experimenting with drugs and alcohol.

A good way to teach your child is to share your daily life with him. Make the stories fit his maturity level, and share with your child events in your life as they happen. In this way, your child can learn through your experiences, and will more readily adopt your value system.

When you turn to God with your problems, let your child know the result of your prayers. Help him understand the

94

comfort you receive by praying. This is an easy way for him to see God working in your daily life.

Another good way to teach a child is by reading to him. This accomplishes several things. You are giving him physical attention, because most children sit on parents' laps when story time comes around; you are giving him focused attention; and he is learning the contents of the book. Bedtime is usually the best time for reading, especially for working parents who must make every minute count.

Include stories other than Christian stories once in a while— especially stories that you make up yourself. My children still remember some of the stories that I made up for them. They almost always asked for one of "Daddy's stories" before we finally turned out the lights.

Story time is one of the best times of the day for close fellowship with your child. I always advise parents with whom I counsel to take a few minutes at bedtime with each child. Share the problems and the joys of the day, read to him, and then pray with him. You are not only enriching your child's emotional being, but you are enriching his intellectual being by choosing informative, educational, and interesting stories.

One parent told me that she wanted to get acquainted with some of the classics, so she brought a couple of books home from the library. Then she invited her husband and fourteen-year-old son into the family room and offered to read these stories aloud. "You can imagine a fourteen-year-old allowing his mother to read to him," she said. "But I struck a bargain with him. I told him that if he would listen for just thirty minutes, he could leave after that. Since it was a snowy day with nothing much else to do, he agreed. After the thirty minutes were up, I told him he could go, but he stayed."

"Oh, well, as long as I'm here, I might as well listen to the ending," he said, twisting in his chair. "You'd probably get mad if I left anyway."

This is a very wise mother. She not only enriched her own mind, but was able to bring her family together for a few winter evenings.

"We received many benefits from that experience," she concluded. "We gained knowledge, and felt a keen sense of love and caring for each other as the reading sessions began to end in discussions of the stories we had read."

This mother was lucky that her teenager became involved. Her story points out that children always have a need to feel loved by their parents, but as they mature, they also need to know that they can have their own way about some things.

Imagine the consequences of starting a family story time very early in the life of your child. There is no end to the benefits the entire family would receive from it.

### It's Never Too Soon to Start

It is vital to the quality of your child's life that you spend time with him during his young years, when he is so willing and pliable. It is a time when he is more positive in his attitude toward you. *It is the very best time to teach spirituality.* Children very much enjoy learning spiritual things, and their attendance in Sunday School and church will continue their spiritual learning process. It will enhance what you are teaching them at home.

Early learning experiences remain with children throughout their lifetimes. And if you are consistent and caring, and always give your child unconditional love, he is well on his way to becoming a strong, self-confident teenager and adult.

Recently, an acquaintance of mine took a college course on the Old Testament. It had been forty years since she had attended summer Bible school as a child, but what she had learned forty years earlier had stayed with her.

One requirement on the course's final exam was to list the

names of the Old Testament books and list the Ten Command-
ments. All this information was still with her from her Bible
school lessons so long ago. Why? First, because she is a Christian and through the years has had this information before her,
and secondly, because her mind was so pliable and receptive
when it was first presented to her.

Parental spiritual values imparted to young children will stay
with them over the years. I am reminded of the story of a POW
from the Vietnam War who spent seven years in captivity in
North Vietnam. As the weeks dragged into months, he began to
pull Bible verses and hymns from his memories of Sunday
School, just to keep his mind busy. Soon, this daily mental
exercise helped him reestablish his relationship with God. This
young captain had not been a practicing Christian as an adult,
but his background of Christian teachings sustained him through
seven years of imprisonment.

Now your child may not decide to go back to college when he
is fifty years old, and I pray that he will not be a prisoner of war.
The object of telling about these two totally different people is
to point out why it is imperative to the spiritual life of your child
that you instill these values at an early age.

An interesting fact about learning is that the atmosphere
surrounding the learning experience plays a great part in how
well the information is received and retained. Children who are
taught in a loving atmosphere not only remember the messages
but usually can tell you something about the person or the
location involved.

Recently, a young, single, working mother of two came into
my office. "You know, Dr. Campbell, I am so afraid that I will
not be able to give my daughters the same kind of life that I had.
My mother didn't work, and she and I would spend a few
minutes at the breakfast table each morning just talking.

"I can still remember that kitchen and my mother's attitude as
she cleared the table for our visits. When I was very small, she

spent these times teaching me the alphabet and my numbers. She taught me how to draw and use watercolors. And as I grew older, she and I discussed everything from dress patterns to dating.

"I think those mornings spent with her were some of the most beneficial learning experiences of my life."

This young mother had made an appointment with me because she was worried about helping her children develop into productive, self-confident adults. I suggested to her that she take some time from her daily schedule and reserve it for some focused attention for her daughters.

I agreed with her that it would be difficult, but once done, the benefits would far outweigh the extra effort spent. Focused attention in a loving atmosphere develops self-esteem, which is extremely important to the overall well-being of your child. You just can't give him too much positive, loving attention. And, of course, a happy, confident child is more than receptive to his parents' spiritual values.

As we close this chapter, and delve into the complexities of teenagers, I want to remind you again that these are the good years to lay a strong foundation. Children are like sponges. They tend to soak up all that surrounds them. So, it stands to reason that if they receive positive emotional, physical, intellectual, and spiritual experiences during these early years, they are more likely to grow up to be healthy adults in every sense of the word.

Unconditional love is crucial. Infants who receive little more than routine physical care are slower in reaching almost every developmental milestone. They are prone to developing emotional problems which inhibit their overall growth and limit their potential. They usually become angry, dissatisfied adults, incapable of accepting their parents' spiritual values.

If your child knows that he is loved, he is sure to want to follow your example throughout his life because of his respect for you. So, you must be very careful to be a good model in every area of his life, not just the spiritual area.

A few years ago, some friends of ours announced the arrival of a son after fifteen years of marriage. Of all the cards and wishes for happiness received, the following poem (which the father keeps on his desk) was the most appreciated. I do not know who wrote it, but I think it is a most appropriate ending to this chapter.

## A Little Fellow Follows Me

A careful man I want to be—
A little fellow follows me;
I do not dare to go astray,
For fear he'll go the self-same way.

I cannot once escape his eyes;
Whate'er he sees me do, he tries;
Like me he says he's going to be—
The little fellow who follows me.

He thinks that I am good and fine—
Believes in every word of mine;
The base in me he must not see—
The little fellow who follows me.　·

I must remember as I go,
Through summer's sun and winter's snow,
I am building for the years that be,
For that little chap who follows me!

# 8

# Teenagers Know Much More Than You Think

*"Be completely humble and gentle; be patient, bearing with one another in love" (Ephesians 4:2).*

When your child becomes a teenager, the day of reckoning is at hand. If you have consistently given him unconditional love and good examples, and taught by life and letter Christian values and principles, your responsibility to your budding adolescent will be much easier; continue being a good example, and keep his emotional tank full. These things, coupled with firm guidelines and patience, will see you and your child through the next four or five difficult years.

Your teenager is no longer the child who believes in every word you say and every move you make. Even though you have surrounded him with unconditional love, he is still going to question you. Yes, even if things have gone relatively well throughout your child's early years, the magic age of thirteen and the adolescent attitude of "No! I won't do it!" arrive.

This is where firm, loving rules and patience come in. Your teen is going to question you because the Creator gave him the drive to establish his own identity. Gradually through these next few years, he will be learning how to leave the nest, and "it ain't easy, McGee!"

## Teenagers Know Much More Than You Think

The other evening, I opened a newspaper to a picture of a father standing beside a six-foot sign which read, "For sale, one set of encyclopedias—never used. Teenage son knows everything!" An amusing way to sell encyclopedias, yes, but the irony of the story is that your teen *does* know everything, that is, practically everything about *you*; that is important.

By the time your child is an adolescent, he knows exactly how you think and what you think. He knows that you want him to adopt your spiritual values; he knows that you want him to make good grades; he knows what makes you angry; he knows what makes you glad.

### Reducing Schoolwork Skirmishes

Nagging your teenager about anything that you want him to do will only succeed in making him angry. The angrier he becomes, the less likely he will be to do what you want. Your best option is to set firm rules that all in your household can live with, and help your teen abide by these rules.

For instance, homework must be done before 'bedtime. Your teen knows that. It was the rule for his older brother, and he knows it is the rule for him. The worst thing you can do is start reminding him every half hour that he should do his homework. Flared tempers and poor homework are about the only results of this action. Telling him every few minutes that he must do his homework is like telling him that the earth is round—he already knows it, and he's going to get mighty tired of hearing it.

Imagine you and your son on his thirteenth birthday. All his guests are standing around waiting for him to blow out the candles, and you pull him aside. Putting your arm around his shoulder, you say, "Son, the earth is round. I want you to remember that."

"Sure, Dad, I already know that." Then he will blow out the candles and try to continue on with his party, but you interrupt him again and say, "I know you know that, Son, but I just want you to remember it."

"OK, Dad, I'll remember it."

The very next day, you approach your son and say to him again, "Say, Son, the earth is round. You got that?"

"Yeah, Dad, you told me that yesterday."

On the third day you say, "Son, I want you to know that the earth is round."

"Good grief, Dad, you've been telling me that for three days now. I know the earth is round. Do you think I'm stupid?"

Imagine how your son would feel if you told him that every day, week in and week out, month in and month out, year in and year out. Pretty soon he wouldn't be able to handle it anymore. He would become destructively angry.

I'll tell you how we handle the homework issue at our house. Usually right after our evening meal, I pick a moment when the boys are in good moods, and ask them about their homework, saying something like, "You guys have any homework this evening?"

The answer is usually, "Yeah, plenty."

"OK, just get it done before bedtime," I reply, keeping the tone upbeat and pleasant. Then I don't say anymore about it. If they need any help, I give it to them, but I don't give them the answers. I usually read through the information they've been given to study, and suggest where they might find an answer.

You are accomplishing two goals when you use this attitude with your child toward his homework. You are not making him angry by making an issue of the given situation, and you are teaching him that he must take the responsibility for his homework.

If you have been taking an authoritarian approach to your teenager's schoolwork and switch to a more authoritative one, he might not pick up on the responsibility of doing his homework immediately. A "dead time" will occur when neither your

102

teen nor you is taking the responsibility. This is usually the time when most parents drop the ball and stand over their child until the work is done. Don't give up.

Your teen's grades may go down initially—he may even fail the course, but stand firm and be patient. When your teen finally realizes that his grades are his responsibility, he will assume that responsibility.

In this area, the 25 percenters and the 75 percenters are really different. The 75 percenters try to get away with all they can, because they don't have the tendency to please. So if you handle the situation in the right way (i.e., no static), the 75 percenter will feel no pressure, but do only what he has to to get by. The 25 percenter, on the other hand, will tend to simply pick up the total responsibility for his homework without an argument.

Take my David, my 75 percenter, for example. He is a bright young man, no learning disabilities, and yet during his seventh, eighth, and ninth grades, he made no better than average grades. But I didn't pressure him, because I knew that one day that kid was going to have to take the responsibility for his own grades. I knew that it was impossible for me to *make* him responsible.

I realize that it is very difficult for parents to understand that they cannot make their teenager responsible, but they can't. The *only* way to create a responsible attitude in your teen is not to take his responsibilities on yourself, but to be an example for your teenager to follow.

Back to David. Like a classic 75 percenter, he maintained a grade average just high enough to allow him to participate in sports and other extracurricular activities. Then one day, his sister asked, "David, have you decided where you are going to college?"

"No, not yet," he replied with little apparent interest. Shortly thereafter, a friend, who was a senior at the time, told David that he was going to Yale the following year.

103

"Hey, that's great! What kind of grade average do you have to have to get in there?"

"Oh, about a 3.5," his friend answered.

At that point, David looked at his report card and saw a GPA of about 2.2. This went on for a couple of semesters, and a few more of his senior friends began discussing where they were going to college. David began to realize, on his own, that he was going to have to take the responsibility of improving his grades if he was going to get to do what he wanted to do in life. WHAMO! The grades started inching upward. He now makes good grades, and hopefully will for the rest of his life. Incidentally, he was accepted by the college of his choice.

That's how most 75 percenters learn responsibility. And it's the same pattern with spirituality, exactly the same.

If we keep telling our kids every day that the earth is round, we are going to make them madder and madder and madder. We must avoid pressuring them; then they will adopt our values. We may not think so at times, but they *will* adopt our values in due time.

We must keep our teenager's emotional tank full, and keep living lives filled with spiritual values. And we must be patient with his outbursts. As we discussed in chapter 5, it is crucial that the adolescent keep his anger coming out of his mouth, and that he learns to exhibit his anger in more positive ways.

## Failure Is Not a Dirty Word

The danger in teenagers knowing how and what we think is that we can transmit our negative attitudes to them just as easily as they learn our positive values.

For example, how do you accept failure when it happens to you, your spouse, or your child? Far too often, failure is seldom discussed in today's families. A typical reaction to failure is evident in the following story about Ryan's report card. His aunt had stopped by for a visit, and his mother proudly told her Ryan's grades. "He made an A and two B's," she told Aunt Janice. "We're so proud of those grades."

"But, Mom, I also made a . . . " but Ryan couldn't finish his sentence because his mother interrupted him.

"Ryan, would you mind getting your Aunt Janice more coffee? It's in the kitchen."

What Ryan wanted to say was that his mother hadn't read the full report card. He had a C on it too.

In Ryan's home, failure is not discussed. We gleam with pride as we discuss family and individual accomplishments, but little is said about failures. When we as parents discuss our own childhoods with our children, we recount with pride our youthful achievements, somehow never getting around to the mistakes we made.

Keeping in mind that teenagers know exactly what we think and what we expect of them, shouldn't we expect them to encounter failure once in a while? Shouldn't we expect them to learn to accept failure as well as success as a fact of life?

One very athletic, accomplished father brought to me a very unhappy, withdrawn, and depressed fourteen-year-old son. The father had told me over the phone that he was a single parent with custody of his son.

"He won't try anything anymore," the obviously self-confident father told me. The boy stood, head down, beside his father.

"Come on in and sit down. Let's get comfortable. Do you like sports, Don?"

"No, I'm not very good at any kind of sports. I played baseball for a while, but didn't do so hot."

"He just quit," the father broke in. "I told him that he could never succeed at anything if he kept on being a quitter."

I looked at the father and said, "I'd like to talk with Don alone for a while. Would you mind waiting for him?" I opened the door to my office, and directed Don's father to the waiting room.

"Tell me, Don," I inquired as I sat down in a chair next to him, "how do you and your father get along?"

"Not very well, Dr. Campbell. You know, I can't seem to do anything right as far as he is concerned. It's not that he's mean about it; it's just that he doesn't want me to fail. He just throws up his hands and walks away when I do something wrong."

"What do you like to do? Tell me something that you like, Don—not necessarily something that your father would like you to do, but something that you like."

Don sat quietly for a while, his gaze fixed on the floor. Finally, he looked up at me with tears in his eyes and said, "I love to play the piano, but I don't think I'm very good at it. At least my dad never takes the time to listen to me. He wants me to play ball, and I hate it. I'm so sick of trying to play ball because Dad wants me to, and then listening to him after every game, telling me all that I did wrong."

Don started sobbing. "Dad would die if he saw me do this. He says men don't cry, just sissies. Well, Dr. Campbell, it looks like I'm going to be a failure as a man too, because I cry a lot."

"Don, I know that your father loves you very much. I know that, because he wouldn't have brought you to visit me if he didn't care for your well-being. Tell you what, I'd like to talk with him for a little while, alone. Then the three of us will talk together, and start planning some happiness for you and your dad."

"I don't know, Dr. Campbell. You'd better not tell Dad that he has done anything wrong. He hates to lose at anything—he hates being wrong."

The sad part about Don's dad is that he was losing in one of the most important jobs of his life—the job of being a father.

It took some time, but eventually this single parent began to realize what he was doing. "I love that boy so much, Dr.

Campbell, that I just can't stand to see him fail," he told me recently. "I don't want him to have to go through the hurt."

"But you see, Dave," I said to him, "if you accept Don's failures and allow him to do the same, soon he will understand that winning isn't all there is to life, and he'll be able to drop the guilt he feels when he loses. After all, sometimes you win and sometimes you lose. With this attitude, Don can soon begin to feel positive about himself and develop more of an adventurous 'I-can't-wait-to-see-what's-out-there' outlook on life."

After a few weeks of counseling, Don's depression began to lift, and his father, Dave, began to understand his own feelings about failure. Together, they learned to add a touch of humor to some of the losing situations in which they found themselves.

In Dave and Don Wilkins' case, Dave was not developing the whole child. He had been trying to meet Don's physical, intellectual, and spiritual needs, but had only depleted his son's emotional strength. How could Don, who was building up so much hate for his father, ever want to accept his father's spiritual values, or any other adult values for that matter?

Not long ago, I read of a major-league baseball player who feels to this day that he is a failure. Can you imagine that— someone who has achieved major-league status feeling like a failure?

He said that when he was nine or ten years old, he had hit three home runs in one Little League game, before finally striking out in the ninth inning. After the game, he ran to his father, ready to bask in his praise. Instead, his father said, "Son, if you had held your elbow a little higher on the strikeout, I think you might have had a base hit."

As the boy grew to manhood, no matter what he did, those words would come back to him. "Son, if you had held your elbow a little higher . . . you might have. . . . "

Our Father in heaven accepts us with all our faults, never saying, "Son, if you would just . . . "—and we must do the

107

same for our children. Our teenagers know that we want them to win, but we must also let them know that we want them to be happy with themselves. They would never enjoy the exhilaration of winning if they could not measure it against a failure or two.

Teens today are tempted by anything and everything. The only way they can come close to resisting these temptations is by feeling good about themselves. If we have filled their emotional tanks on a daily basis, they have a good start. As in the story of the father telling his son the world is round, we cannot tell our children every day that they can't do this and can't do that. So we must simply set up the ground rules and lovingly guide them to abide by them.

## The Importance of Questions and Doubts

Keeping up an honest, open line of communication is one of the best ways to help your teen abide by your rules. Your teenager many times wants to talk with you about anything and everything—he just doesn't know how to get started. He sometimes wants to talk about moral issues, including sexual morality, faith, and family closeness. He values your input above peer input. He just doesn't know how to go about letting you know this.

Unfortunately, it is difficult for many Christian parents to discuss these things with their teenager. If you are having such a problem, go back to chapter 2 of this book and question your understanding of yourself. When you understand who you are and what makes you feel the way you feel, you will be better able to talk with your teen.

I have found the very best place for talking is in a car. Every time our family takes a vacation, my teenagers and I get into some interesting conversations.

I just ride along, saying nothing. If there is anything a teen gets uneasy about, it's silence—especially when a parent says nothing. Soon, he starts talking. If you are patient enough, and just answer his questions, not taking on a "preachy" attitude, he will soon get to the real reason he started the conversation. It is during these times that your topics of conversation can run from why babies cry at two in the morning, to dating, and to spirituality. Vacations are wonderful times to get acquainted with your teenager.

Your teenager knows you want him to accept your faith, but he is uncomfortable with a restricting God. He needs to see God as One who liberates. He needs to know God's unconditional love and forgiveness. If you tell him only of the God who controls and disciplines, and you start demanding that he believe exactly the way you do, you will lessen the chance of him following your teaching. Your teen must feel free to question and doubt, and arrive at some of his own answers about spirituality.

Your teenager is a wonderful human being. He has arrived at a traumatic time in life and needs your unconditional love and support to get him through these next few years.

When he looks in the mirror, he rarely sees a perfect image looking back at him. He sees someone who is too short or too skinny or someone who has a bad complexion or braces. Couple this with the fact that the Lord has given him the desire to start questioning his parents and anyone else who is in authority, and you have a very interesting person. A person who needs his parents' love and attention, but will not ask for it. A person who loves to have his mother tuck him into bed at night, but will defend to the death his right for privacy in his room. A person who refuses his father's offer to help him write the speech he is going to give during his bid for class presidency, but finds his way to his parents' room when the lights are out, and timidly asks, "Dad, do you have a minute? I want to ask you about a couple of things."

## Kids Who Follow, Kids Who Don't

A very wise minister accepted the challenge of giving a baccalaureate address. He stood before the high school graduating class and said, "I really like teenagers. They are some of the finest people I know. I'm not going to stand here and tell you the world is out there just for the asking, or it's tough out there but you can do it, or life is what you make it. You already know all of that. I am simply going to say that I have faith in you. I know you will make a few mistakes, but I also know that you'll make a lot of right decisions.

"One of you could be President. Another could own a large business. But more than that, what I want for each of you is to be happy with who and what you are, and I pray to God that this will be your main achievement."

It takes a lot of time and patience to get your kids through the rocky teen years. Pat and I still have one teenager at home, and another away in college, and as this minister said, they are among the finest people I know—and the most questioning, I might add.

We must not treat our teens like little children. They know far more about us and the world than we imagine. They are also still learning and seeking their way. Be open to their questioning. Listen to them, with respect for their opinions. Admit it when you don't know something; then say, "Let's try to find the answer together."

Allow your teen to grow as he questions and seeks to become more independent. In a few more years, he too may be a parent. If you have allowed him to be himself, and to become what God wants him to be, he will be way ahead of the game in his own child-rearing.

# 9

# Negativism Will
# Boomerang on You

*"But you have neglected the more important matters of
the law—justice, mercy, and faithfulness. You should
have practiced the latter, without neglecting the former.
You blind guides! You strain out a gnat but swallow a
camel" (Matthew 23:23-24).*

Negative Christianity. Sounds like a contradiction of terms,
doesn't it? After all, isn't Christianity love and peace and joy?
Yes, but all too often, Christian parents use such negative
*approaches* to teaching spiritual values to their children that they
do more harm than good. Christian youth leaders have this same
problem. They often, unintentionally, try to force the young
people in their charge toward a Christian lifestyle instead of
leading them to it. Steve, a youth minister I know, is a perfect
example of this.

Steve is a fine young man who came right out of seminary to
church youth ministry. Unfortunately, when he first arrived, he
didn't know how to reach adolescents.

Steve is a very moralistic 25 percenter. Developing leadership
qualities is more difficult for 25 percenters, so you can imagine
some of the problems they would have leading a group of teens.
Leading teens is difficult enough, even for 75 percenters! One of
Steve's first encounters with his church youth group illustrates
his dilemma.

Steve had invited the teens over to his home. As he stepped

out onto the porch, he overheard several young people gossiping about a new member in the group.

"Ross, they were saying some pretty heavy things about that new girl," Steve told me later. "I angered immediately, went back into the house to get my Bible, and proceeded to give them a long lecture. I was determined to get the upper hand, and teach these kids a thing or two about love and respect for other people."

"How did they react to that, Steve?" I asked. "Did they decide that they would never gossip again, and thank you for the advice?" I knew what Steve's answer was going to be. Of course, they didn't. These kids are naturally somewhat antiauthority, because they are teenagers. The party ground to a screeching halt. They all kept quiet for the rest of the evening—a classic adolescent reaction.

Why did the 25 percenters quiet down? Do you think they were angry? Yes, to some extent, but they were primarily hurt, and felt guilty that they had disappointed their leader.

How about the 75 percenters? They had the same reaction as the 25 percenters, but do you think they felt guilty? No way. The 75 percenters were so mad at Steve they couldn't see straight. The nerve of him trying to tell them what to do in that ultra-moralistic, authoritarian way.

Steve would have been much farther ahead if he had known some basics about the personalities of youth. He needed to know why all the kids reacted essentially the same, why they instinctively felt hurt albeit for different reasons.

To be harsh and negative with a kid that age, or any kid for that matter, will accomplish little. We must learn to be firm but pleasant, consistent but positive. These rules apply to every age group, but are magnified a thousandfold with thirteen- through fifteen-year-olds. That's why we need to start learning as young parents how to handle our children, so that we will know what to do when they reach thirteen.

## Negativism Will Boomerang on You

Steve, the youth minister, made a big mistake by coming down too hard on his kids. The success of the youth meeting was totally destroyed. However, Steve is a sensitive person. He knew immediately that he had done something terribly wrong.

"What should I have done, Ross?"

"Well, you shouldn't have been so negative and harsh. They already knew that they shouldn't gossip. How many times have they heard that before? Telling them not to gossip is like telling them the earth is round. Every teenager knows that the earth is round, but if you ignore that fact and continually tell them that the earth is round, you'll only succeed in making them angry.

"The same thing holds true about telling them not to gossip. It just made your youth group angry, or left some of them with feelings of guilt.

"They knew you were there. You caught them in the act. They were trapped, so they just had to sit there, waiting to see what was going to come out of your mouth. And if anything negative came out of your mouth, that was going to be it. So, you made a negative statement, and that was it. You lost them.

"What you should have said was, 'Anybody want mustard on his hot dog?' In other words, you should have ignored their statements."

The young people in that group knew their leader was upset. They could see it on his face. What he needed to do was to handle the situation meekly. *Meekness* doesn't mean "weak" or "wimpy." *Meekness* means "withholding your power," or "holding your power in reserve." Christ was all-powerful, but He always held it in reserve.

That is the way we want to interact with teenagers. We have the power (and they know it), but we don't have to use it. You see, once we have used our power, then we have nothing. There is no longer any reason for them to respect us.

Steve used his power, and the kids lost respect for him. If he had just held his power in reserve, and been pleasant, things

113

would have been different. He could have played the game, "I know what you kids are doing, and I know that you know that I know. And I know that you know better, so I am trusting you to take care of it yourself."

## Force Is Not the Answer

You see, the opposite of passive-aggressive behavior is learning to take care of things for yourself—to take personal responsibility. You cannot expect kids to grow out of the passive-aggressive stage and take responsibility for themselves unless you give them the opportunity. Anytime you start yelling and screaming, or start lecturing, or become negative with your child or teenager, in his eyes you are telling him that what he has done wrong is *your* responsibility—not his. You are preventing him from taking responsibility for his own behavior.

That is what Steve was doing. He was "preaching" Christianity to his youth group in a negative way by chastising them for gossiping. He was trying to force them to think as he was thinking, and to make amends for their actions.

As a parent, you cannot force your values on your child, especially when he becomes an adolescent. Unconditional love and development of the whole child is the only way to keep him free from inappropriate anger, so that when he reaches adulthood, he will *want* to adopt your values. The responsibility will be his whether or not to follow your spiritual beliefs. He cannot be forced to make that decision.

The main theme of Christian child-rearing "experts" of today is *parental power.* I am not saying that parents should not be in control, and should not set rules. I *am* saying that parental control should be based on love and understanding.

Fill your child's emotional tank. See to his intellectual needs. Help him take care of his physical needs. If you do these things, his spiritual needs will be fulfilled by your daily example and

114

## Negativism Will Boomerang on You

guidance. Displays of force and power will not be necessary.

Not too long ago, I heard a prominent Christian "personality" speak on the subject of getting children back into our churches.

"When my daughter was five years old," he began, "she didn't want to wear a certain dress to Sunday School. So what do you think I did? I stuffed her into the dress, and made her wear it to Sunday School."

"Then," he continued, "when she was fourteen, and decided that she didn't even want to go to Sunday School or church, how do you think I handled that? Well, I used basically the same principle. I stuffed her into the car, and made her go to church!"

I couldn't believe my ears. Just imagine the anger that girl was feeling. Her feelings and needs obviously were not being considered; only her father's need to have her in church and Sunday School was being met.

Don't do this to your child. Don't "stuff" him into Christianity. It simply won't work. No one can be dragged, kicking and screaming, into the kingdom of God. If you have met your child's needs, and you are truly involved in a daily Christian lifestyle, your child will likely follow.

Recently, I had the opportunity to talk with Terri, an eighteen-year-old who was fifteen when her parents became Christians.

"I didn't think it was too bad, Dr. Campbell," she told me. "I had always enjoyed going to church and Sunday School, so the change in my life concerning church attendance wasn't drastic. But there *were* drastic changes in our family life. We could no longer watch television, go to movies, or listen to rock music. My sister Lynn and I even had to quit wearing blue jeans or slacks.

"I went along with it. It was easier to do that than argue with Mom and Dad. But Lynn was a different story. She didn't want any part of it. She hated giving up her tapes and her favorite jeans. It must have been awful for her when Mom and Dad first

115

started going to church. She really rebelled. I remember one time when my cousin invited us to go shopping. When we got far enough away from our house that my folks could no longer see us, Lynn pulled off her skirt and blouse in the car, and there she was in her favorite jeans and T-shirt. I nearly fainted.

"But gradually, Mom and Dad cooled off on some of their restrictions, and our lives got back to normal. I'm so glad things turned out the way they did. I don't think Lynn would have lasted. Now that I look back at it, we were held down so tightly that it was like wearing blinders—you know, those things they put on horses to keep them from seeing anything except the center of the road?

"When I went to college and got out into the world, I realized how very limited my view of life had been. I wondered how Lynn would handle getting away from home. I was afraid that she might be pretty wild and reckless for a while. And so, on my Christmas vacation, I was very glad to see that Mom and Dad had let up somewhat. I think it's the best thing they could have done for Lynn."

Terri is an intelligent young woman. She realized what was happening to her sister. She knew that her parents' demands were causing Lynn to go in exactly the opposite direction.

Terri and Lynn's parents had become Christians when their daughters were at crucial ages. Parental stability is a must in the life of an adolescent. And here were Terri and Lynn's parents going through some tremendous changes. However, they soon saw what negativism was doing to their daughters, and backed off on some of their inappropriately harsh demands.

The movie *Footloose* came to mind when Terri was telling me about her parents. I don't know if you have ever seen that movie, but it is a perfect example of forcing teenagers into a specific lifestyle. The movie has some rough language in it, but it serves only to portray exactly what teenagers will do if they are held down tight enough. They will rebel as the teenagers in

116

*Footloose* rebelled.

The kids in the movie were not allowed to listen to anything but classical music. They were not allowed to dance. They were not even allowed to read anything unless it was sanctioned by a church committee. It is not a true story, but it is a clear example of passive-aggressive behavior and anger.

Teenagers are going to naturally question you and your actions. If you constantly restrict them, and force them to do exactly as you say, you will lose them. The teen years are very trying for parents, but if you have established a strong foundation of love and spiritual basics, you can get them through these years with a minimum of pain.

## The Gentle Nudge of Love

When my wife, Pat, and I lived in California, I met a man who said he and his wife were agnostics. They didn't believe that anyone could know God or His great love. They didn't even believe in love. He explained to me that love between a man and a woman was nothing more than physical attraction. He defined parental love simply as nature's way of assuring continuation of the species.

When their first child was born, this couple decided that if the child wanted to become a Christian, or wanted to form any kind of spiritual beliefs, he would be allowed to make that choice on his own. They vowed they would not interfere. Talk about a negative approach to Christianity! I felt so sorry for them and their son.

One afternoon, when their child was still an infant, Charles and I were talking. "You know, Ross," he said, "Meg and I believe there is no such thing as love, but when we hold that baby, we get the strangest feelings. They are quite difficult to describe."

I couldn't believe what I was hearing. I talked to him of God's love for man, and of man's love for his fellowman, but he just didn't want to hear about it. These were the most unusual people I had ever met.

A few months later, we happened to see each other again, and Charles had quite a revelation to share with me. "Ross, do you remember when I told you about the feelings Meg and I didn't understand when we held our baby? Well, we know what they are—they are love!"

He went on to explain how he and Meg began to feel an emptiness in their lives. They joined a group that was starting a Christian church in their neighborhood. "We have been foolish a lot of years," Charles admitted to me. "We were both raised by parents who did not attend church regularly, but at least they did not deny God."

"How about your son's spiritual life, Charles?" I asked. "Are you still going to let him make that decision on his own?"

"Well, we won't force him into anything. We hope he will see how Meg and I feel about our faith and follow our example. We certainly do not want him to experience the void which was present in our lives during the past few years."

Parents with a mistaken liberal attitude of noninfluence can do as much damage to children as parents who try to force their spiritual beliefs on their children. It is dangerous to leave young people totally void of spiritual values. Luke 6:49 tells us what will happen if we do not give our children a foundation of unconditional love, and if we do not allow them to see us live our faith daily: "But the one who hears My words and does not put them into practice is like a man who built a house on the ground without a foundation. The moment the torrent struck that house, it collapsed and its destruction was complete."

When children are very young, it is easy to teach them about God. They are trusting and eager to learn. But as they enter the teen years, when they naturally become antiauthority about everything, spirituality is one more thing they question. Adolescents want to hear of a loving, forgiving God.

Just think about it. God placed in these wonderful young people the desire to question authority. So how can this desire be wrong? If you squelch this natural need in 75 percenters, and only give them the doctrine of an angry God who will strike them down at any given moment, you will lose these kids for sure. This same doctrine taught to 25 percenters will frighten them, make them feel guilty, and in many cases, if it is strong enough, will do serious psychological damage. Children and teens need to know the loving, forgiving God as well as the God of justice and righteousness.

## The Error of "Doomsday" Parenting

We also must guard ourselves against the "Pharisee" attitude with our children, especially our teenagers. The Pharisees were good men. They were educated and sincere, but they were so convinced of the absolute rightness of their point of view and their personal experiences that they could not accept even the Saviour Himself.

Parents are so used to being the major authority figures in their children's lives that they all too often overreact in negative ways to the questioning attitudes of their adolescents. They hand out guilt—"How could you embarrass your mother like that?" (Imagine what that statement does to the 25 percenter.) They hand out "hellfire and damnation" theology—"That music is straight from the devil, and if you listen to it . . . ." And they hand out doomsday teaching—"If you don't do as I say, God will punish you!"

Some of the most serious cases I see are adolescents who have been "threatened with God." Parents who sincerely care about the spiritual life of their children but mistakenly take the negative approach actually can and do cause serious emotional problems.

## Kids Who Follow, Kids Who Don't

"You'll-do-God's-bidding-or-die-and-go-to-hell" child-rearing will affect 75 percenters and 25 percenters differently. Seventy-five percenters will build up a sweltering anger, and go just as far in the opposite direction as they can just as soon as they can.

Twenty-five percenters, on the other hand, will be scared to death and develop strong guilt feelings. When constantly subjected to Christian negativism, they will become obsessive and injured psychologically. Instead of experiencing the comfort and love of God, they are likely to live in anxiety and fear. Their tendency to low self-esteem will dip even lower.

Sixteen-year-old Brian Starks was brought to me by his parents. I noticed immediately that he stayed very close to his mother. He also appeared to be extremely anxious. Brian's parents were unusually strict. They demanded that Brian and his fourteen-year-old brother, Brady, attend every church function with them.

As I began to counsel this family, I learned that Brady was an extreme 75 percenter. I could see that he was doing what his parents asked of him concerning church attendance, but I couldn't help but wonder if the Starks knew what was in store for them when Brady got a little older.

Gradually, Brian poured out his story. "You see, Dr. Campbell, I've always been, I guess, jealous of Brady. He seems to be able to do anything. He's smart. He can really play a trumpet, and he's quite a runner. I guess that's where the trouble started.

"A couple of weeks before the big spring track meet, Brady began to tease me. I hate it when he brags about everything he can do. He knows I'm not an athlete. Anyway, he just kept on teasing me. Finally, I told him to shut up and I put my fingers in my ears so I wouldn't have to listen. Then I prayed that Brady would get hurt somehow, just enough to keep him out of the meet.

"Two days later, he went out with some rough guys, and was

in a car wreck, and broke his leg. I felt awful. I knew that God was going to punish me for causing Brady to break his leg. It was right after that that I began to see the Grim Reaper at my bedroom door. Honestly, every night he was there. I thought that God had sent him to take me because of how I felt about Brady. It was awful."

Brian suffered severe emotional damage because of the "God-will-punish-you-if-you-don't . . . " attitude at home. It will take some time to help him through this, but I have hopes. I am always sad when I have a patient like Brian. He's an intelligent boy; he is just as musically talented as his brother, but his 25-percenter personality coupled with low self-esteem and a negative approach to Christianity has cost him a great deal.

## Finding a Middle Ground

It is all too easy to veer into overstrict or overpermissive methods of dealing with your children. I know. Sometimes I think if I could just tell my kids no to everything, then I wouldn't have anything to worry about. I would know where they were all the time.

I, and all other parents of teenagers, know that is impossible. We wouldn't really want it for our children. The middle road is where we must walk with our teens. After we have filled their emotional tanks; after we have gotten acquainted with each of them individually; then we can interact with them in meaningful and fruitful ways.

As I suggested to Steve, the youth minister, when you're tempted to "lower the boom," just cool it and change the subject. Don't get all bent out of shape at their negative actions. The more *negative* reaction they get from you, the more *negative* action they will give you. Relax, fellow parents—enjoy your precious teenager—the negative and the positive. It won't be long until you will have a young adult in your house who'll say,

# Kids Who Follow, Kids Who Don't

"Hey, how about me driving to church today, and treating you all to dinner out afterward!"

# 10

# "Special" Children Can Be Helped

*"The King will reply, 'I tell you the truth, whatever you did for one of the least of these brothers of mine, you did for me'" (Matthew 25:40).*

James was a happy little kid. From the time he was born through his seventh year, he didn't appear to have any unusual problems. He walked when he was supposed to. He talked at the right time. He was easy to potty train. To the casual observer and even to his schoolteachers, he was an average, everyday kid.

No one realized that he was memorizing everything in order to get through each school day. But James' mother is a very sensitive person. She knew that something was wrong with her child; she just couldn't find anyone who would agree with her and tell her what it was.

Everyone said, "Oh, boys will be boys."

Still, she felt that something was wrong. Toward the end of second grade, James began to be hard to manage. He often accused his mother of not really loving him. He argued with her constantly. She never felt that she was really communicating with him in a comfortable, maternal, child-bonding way.

When James entered the third grade, he started having academic problems. He just couldn't keep up with the other kids, because learning was going from general concepts into an abstract level. James just couldn't seem to understand. He was still trying to memorize everything. And as a consequence, his grades started going down.

Out of utter desperation, he put more and more energy into academics because he was basically a good kid and wanted to do well. And for about a month or two, he did do very well. Then his total energy output completely exhausted him and his grades started down again. He panicked and became depressed.

James' concentration power waned. He couldn't remember simple tasks. He became a behavior problem at school and at home. He even began having little quirky movements of his body, which were so well hidden that no one really recognized what they were. For instance, he let his hair grow long to make it seem he was flipping it from his eyes when actually he was nervously jerking his head. He shuffled his feet when he walked, making clicking sounds with his heels. He barely made it through third grade.

When the fourth grade started, he just couldn't keep up. His behavior worsened; he became more defiant and harder to manage. He began to have temper tantrums. At this point, his parents brought him to me for counseling.

After we evaluated him, we found a very depressed child with extremely low self-esteem. He was self-critical, and felt unconsciously that nobody cared about him—that nobody really loved him.

He was filled with pent-up anger, especially toward authority. That passive-aggressiveness was exhibiting itself in misbehavior toward the number-one authority in his life—his parents, and toward lower authorities—his schoolteachers.

There were several reasons why James' grades were going down. Number one, he had perceptual problems. In other words, the information coming into his mind, as it was processed, became somewhat distorted. Therefore, his studies were confusing to him. Secondly, he was depressed, and depression

124

can either create or intensify a learning problem, because con-centration is so difficult for a depressed person. Thirdly, he was handicapped due to his passive-aggressive behavior. He was getting back at authority by purposely, but unconsciously (that is to say it was out of his awareness) making poor grades. He was getting back at the chief authority figures in his life—his teach-ers and his parents.

This good-looking lad was doing poorly in every area of his life. His learning difficulties had developed into a total life problem.

His antiauthority attitude was out of hand. Even at his age, he was against everything his parents stood for, including spiritual-ity. He hated church. He hated his Sunday School teacher. He was a constant disruption in his Sunday School class.

We began treating James for depression. We counseled his parents to deal with his anger by encouraging him to get it out from inside where it was destroying him. And after taking these steps, we got him the academic help he needed.

After about four or five months of therapy, he was doing well. His behavior was improved, and for the first time in his life, he was able to be an affectionate child. For the first time, his parents could really manifest their love toward him, and he could accept it.

It was the first time he would let them love him, because now affection was pleasant to him. He could really believe that they meant it, because finally, he was experiencing positive self-worth. He was beginning to develop a positive self-image.

We involved an educational therapist in James' treatment to take away the passive-aggressive, anti-learning attitude that had grown within him. This took the responsibility for his education out of his parents' hands. They were no longer involved in tutoring him.

First, the educational therapist created a positive personal relationship with James. Then she built on that relationship, and turned it into a positive attitude toward academics. She worked with his teachers at school, and got him into the special education programs that he needed. She helped his teachers understand how to help him feel good about himself and continue his positive attitude toward academics.

With his anger subsiding and his depression lifting with therapy, James became less passive-aggressive and less anti-authority. Now, for the first time, he became pliable and receptive to spiritual values and teaching.

James is fortunate. His mother is a perceptive Christian who wouldn't take a "boys will be boys" answer to her son's problem. And when the problem was finally diagnosed, both she and her husband made a concentrated and sincere effort toward solving it. Now, with patience and time, and by Christian example in their daily living, James' parents will be able to help him develop into a well-rounded adult who will want to follow their spiritual values.

## Insights on the Handicapped

Children with perceptual handicaps or chronic medical problems have the same problems as average children. The sad thing about these children is that along with the normal everyday problems, they must deal with their own particular handicap.

These special children tend to be antiauthority in every way, including anti-spirituality. They are prone to wrongdoing, even criminal acts. A recent study of perceptually handicapped males shows that adolescents with diagnosed perceptual handicaps are more likely to become involved in juvenile delinquency. The odds of being judged delinquent are 220 percent greater for these young people than for their nonhandicapped peers.

These children are usually quite depressed. Depression is the one thing that we desperately want to avoid in all children and teenagers. The more depressed a child is, the more angry he

# "Special" Children Can Be Helped

becomes. Depression produces anger. And angry children are much more likely to be passive-aggressive.

When we take this already depressed and passive-aggressive child, and superimpose the normal depression and normal passive-aggressive behavior of adolescence, we have a kid who is profoundly depressed and profoundly passive-aggressive.

Long before we can teach spirituality to this child, we have to help him through his anger and depression. We have to try to understand his particular problem, and let him know that we love him unconditionally. Then, and only then, are we on the road to helping him understand his need for a personal relationship with Jesus Christ.

Our educational system has become more adept at identifying the child with perceptual problems. We are now in a position to better understand and help this child, but there are many other people who are still unaware of his dilemma. Unfortunately, they think the perceptually handicapped child is lazy or stubborn or just plain dumb. They do not understand that the child does not perceive or take information from his environment through his senses to his mind in the same way that an average child does. This child's understanding of the world around him is distorted due to a neurological problem usually present from birth.

Imagine the child's dilemma. He has trouble academically which creates anger in him. This anger is created from two sources—the child himself because he cannot understand the work, and the parent who nags because he is not doing the work. Therefore, he doesn't feel understood or loved by his parents, causing more anger and depression. He doesn't get along with his peers, so the end result is an extremely depressed child. By the time he reaches adolescence, this depression will likely result in severe behavioral and emotional disorders.

One afternoon last summer, I attended my son Dale's baseball game. I recognized Matt, a member of the opposing team. He and his parents had been in to see me earlier that spring. Matt is perceptually handicapped. He is thirteen years old and the neighborhood problem kid.

I found a seat next to Matt's adult neighbor, Larry, just as Matt was coming up to bat.

"Hey, Larry," Matt called, "which side of the base is the right side? I think I bat right-handed. That kid that just batted is left-handed. Should I stand where he did?"

"No, Matt," Larry answered impatiently. "You should stand on the other side of the plate."

Larry turned to me. "Isn't that the dumbest thing? Matt doesn't know the right side from the left side of home plate."

"Maybe he has some learning problems," I offered.

"He sure does. If he wasn't so blamed ornery, he could learn!"

"No, really, Larry," I continued, "there are people who don't know left from right."

"That's impossible. There's nothing wrong with that kid that a little willow switch now and then can't cure!"

Poor Matt. Besides the normal anxieties of competing, he has the added frustration of perceptual problems and a not so understanding neighbor. Fortunately, his parents and his school have recognized his problems and are helping him.

It is critical that the parents of these special children fill their kids' emotional tanks daily. All too often, a perceptually handicapped child has great difficulty understanding our positive feelings for him. For this reason, he needs extra helpings of love, physical contact, and focused attention from the important people in his life.

To convey love, we use eye contact (visual perception is needed), physical contact (an overwhelmingly complex sense), and focused attention (requires seeing, hearing, and the possession of a certain amount of logic). If a perceptual problem exists in any of these areas, the child's understanding is distorted, thus creating overwhelming frustration for both the child and us, not

128

to mention lack of communication.

## A Child's Pain Is the Parent's Pain

Not only does the handicapped child experience pain and frustration, but so do his parents. They usually run through a whole gamut of emotions before they can come to grips with the fact that their child is suffering from learning disabilities.

They begin by denying that the problem exists, which, in itself, heightens the child's frustration. They take the child to therapists for second and third opinions; they isolate themselves, thinking no one understands their pain.

Then they start on a heavy guilt trip. They feel that they caused their child's problem. They question their child-rearing methods: "Were we too strict?" "Were we too easy-going?" Anger is usually next. "We're surely not the guilty persons in this situation. We've done everything we can. It must be that the doctor doesn't know what he's talking about. And this neighborhood and this school—nobody knows what's going on!"

Parents finally start blaming each other. When the child sees this, he experiences fear and more depression.

At this point, the parents who really want to help their child will commit themselves to counseling. Here they will learn that there is still hope. They will find how to deal with their child's specific problem, and how and where to reach for educational assistance. Soon they will be removing some of the reasons for depression and anger from the child.

Rick, a handsome, dark-eyed, ten-year-old, walked into my office, keeping well ahead of his mother, Joyce.

"I sure hope you can find out what is wrong, Dr. Campbell," he said, "because my mother worries a lot about me. Sometimes she even cries. I hate to see her do that. Maybe you can tell her something today that will make her feel better."

Joyce was a single parent. Her husband had left her just a year ago—the same time that Rick's problem began to surface at school. She was a sincere mother who tried to do everything she could for Rick. The teacher at Rick's school had told her that there really wasn't anything wrong with him. Rick's only problem, she said, was too much maternal attention.

"You're trying too hard to compensate for the absence of his father, Joyce, and you're spoiling him. He can read. He's just being stubborn to get all the attention he can," the teacher stated firmly.

And so, armed with this information, Joyce gave Rick less attention, and tutored him every night after school. Nothing worked. His behavior problem increased, and his grades dropped to failing. It was at this point that Joyce brought him to me.

After we had evaluated him, I called Rick and his mother into my office.

"Well, Rick, we'll just see what we can do to make your mother and you feel better."

I went over the tests with them, and showed them that Rick had a visual perceptual problem and a slight attention deficit. "But don't worry, you're a bright boy, Rick. And I doubt that you are too stubborn to try to read. I think you're all right, and I'm going to try to help you."

Rick's eyes lit up. "Listen to that, Mom. I'm not dumb after all. You don't have to worry so much about me now."

In Rick's case, he was feeling very responsible for his mother's unhappiness. Joyce was wise to seek counseling. In doing so, she became aware of his true problem, and he was able to get rid of some of the guilt which also caused some of his depression.

Joyce had gone through all of the frustration that other parents encounter when dealing with a perceptually handicapped child. All of these feelings are normal. The problem with them lies in the possibility that some parents will stay in one of these phases too long, increasing the child's negative feelings of self-worth.

The problems of most perceptually handicapped children can

be minimized if they are caught soon enough. James and Rick are fortunate because their parents caught their problems in time. Catching the problem "in time" means catching it before the child becomes an adolescent.

When the problem remains untreated by the age of thirteen, fourteen, or fifteen, the child usually experiences much more than academic difficulties. His problems almost always include drugs, sex, lying, stealing, running away, or even suicide attempts.

In telling the stories of James, Matt, and Rick, I have tried to help you understand the dilemmas of perceptually handicapped children. It is obvious that their problems, coupled with the normal rough spots of life, can pose a real threat to their overall well-being, including their spirituality. Developing these learning disabled children into whole children takes more time, patience, and understanding, but it *can* be done.

## Kids with Chronic Illnesses

Perceptual deficits are not the only problems that affect the behavior of children. Chronic medical problems can also create emotional and behavioral controversies. We can become so involved in the daily physical needs of a chronically ill child (daily correct doses of insulin, for example), that we overlook his emotional needs.

As physically impaired children grow older, they become increasingly bitter about their disease or handicap. They become angry with caring parents, because the parents have inadvertently replaced the natural giving of love with daily medical attention. These kids can become defiant, not only toward their parents, but toward all authority.

Take Linda Walker, who her mother described to me as "a fussy baby from the beginning."

"We tried everything we could think of, but we just couldn't

131

seem to make her happy. Then, when she was three, the pediatrician discovered that she had a chronic heart defect. From then until now, our life with her has been one trip after another to specialists."

"How is her physical health at the present?" I asked the Walkers.

"It's stabilized right now," Paul Walker answered, "but her pregnancy certainly won't help her any."

"I see you have one other child, a son," I noted as I scanned their file. "How is his health?"

"Oh, it's just perfect," Mrs. Walker answered. "We're so proud of Jeff. He's a fine athlete, and quite an accomplished pianist."

"Has Linda ever developed any hobbies?"

"No," her father answered. "We've been so busy attending to her health problems that we never had the time to do much else with her. Don't get me wrong, it's not that we didn't want to. She has always been such a cranky kid that we never could talk her into doing anything other than going to school. And now, here she is pregnant. I guess it's too late."

"At least she is going to marry the father of the baby next week," Mrs. Walker added. "Maybe that'll make her happy. We've done all we know to do, Dr. Campbell, but we surely went wrong someplace. She's been very depressed lately. I'm relieved that we talked her into coming to see you. I sure hope you can get through to her. She's in a sorry frame of mind to start a marriage."

"Why don't both of you wait outside, and let me talk with Linda," I suggested as I ushered the Walkers toward the door.

Curled up in a chair in the corner of the waiting room was Linda—seventeen years old and pregnant.

"Would you like to come in, Linda?" I asked as I walked over to her.

"Why not? That's what they brought me here for." As she sat

down in a chair in my office, she said with a frown, "I don't know what good my being here is going to do. You can't change things."

"You're right, Linda; I can't change things, but maybe in time I can help you to change the way you feel about some things."

When Linda began to open up, my suspicions were confirmed. She was a classic example of the chronically ill child whose parents spent so much time caring for her physical needs that they forgot about her emotional needs.

"Jeff can do this—Jeff can do that! That's all I ever heard. 'Let's go to Jeff's ball game, Linda. It'll do you good to get out of the house. Let's go to Jeff's piano recital, Linda. Maybe you'll decide to start taking piano lessons.' And you should see the grades Jeff makes—straight A's. I made C's and I think that's plenty good enough."

I've just started counseling with Linda, but I feel she can be helped with her depression. I know that her parents love her. They didn't realize that they had been substituting emotional attention with medical attention. Linda's low grades and her pregnancy both were subconscious acts of defiance against this seeming indifference.

There are other reasons why chronically ill children become depressed and bitter, but in my years of treating these children, I have found two principal pitfalls for parents. They are the ones we just discussed: a substitution of medical attention for emotional fulfillment, and lack of behavioral control and firmness.

Parents of chronically ill children feel such pity and sometimes even blame and guilt that they do not try to normally control the child's behavior. This results in a manipulative child who will use his illness to control his parents.

As we saw in the story of James, success can come. If the problem is detected and help is obtained in time, both the parent and the child will benefit beyond measure. The child will not only be able to handle academics, but will be able to feel worthy of the love of his parents and friends.

Once he has gone through the normal antiauthority years of adolescence, he will follow his parents' spiritual values, not only because they want him to, but because he wants to.

# 11

# The Deteriorating Family

*"Better a meal of vegetables where there is love than a fattened calf with hatred" (Proverbs 15:17).*

Mark Johnson sat across from me, impatiently tapping his well-manicured fingers on the arm of his chair. He was obviously a person of financial means. His overall appearance and his mannerisms were flawless. His lovely wife, Brenda, whose attire and behavior appeared equally as perfect, seemed equally as impatient.

"Sorry to keep you waiting," I began as I finished scanning their file. "I see you are an attorney, Mark. My son-in-law is an attorney. I really admire you guys. There appears to be no end to the details you have to pursue before finally presenting your case.

"And how are you, Brenda? Is the world of children's clothing keeping you busy?" Brenda is the owner and operator of a fashionable children's clothing store.

Both Mark and Brenda are Sunday School teachers and are active in a large church. All outward indications give them the mark of a very successful couple. They have two children, a daughter Amy, age six, and a son Todd, age eleven.

So why are they sitting in my office?

"Dr. Campbell, we need to talk to you about Todd. Six months ago, he seemed to change from a normal boy into a quiet stranger who was angry all the time. He constantly found excuses to stay away from us. Goodness knows, we have very little time to spend with each other as it is. Mark's work load seems to be increasing daily, and my shop keeps me past 10 o'clock many evenings," Brenda began.

"Yes, Dr. Campbell," Mark agreed, "and you'd think that the kids would appreciate all that we can give them because we work all those long hours. Amy hasn't given us any trouble, but Todd is a different story.

"A few nights ago, some of his older friends brought him home drunk. What in the world would make an eleven-year-old kid who has everything do such a thing?"

"We're shocked beyond words," added Brenda. "And to make matters worse, he's disrupted the entire household schedule with this silly trick. Mark had to reschedule his clients, and I'm taking time away from the store to keep this appointment with you. Don't get me wrong, we want to help Todd, but we can't understand why this happened. As Mark said, we've given him everything, and this is the way he thanks us."

"What in the world is wrong with our boy, Dr. Campbell?" Mark said as he began to pace the floor. "Or could it be us? I can settle legal matters of the most important people in this city, but I can't make my own son happy."

Yes, what is wrong? Why would an eleven-year-old use alcohol on a regular basis? I found, as I counseled the Johnsons, that Todd had used alcohol many times, but was able to conceal it from his parents before now.

Why is there an increase in the number of fifth-graders who are trying drugs and alcohol? Why did 57 percent of a group of ninth-graders in a recent survey state that they had used alcohol more than once in the past twelve months? Why did this same study (of predominantly Christian youths) reveal that almost

136

twice as many fifth-graders reported experimentation with alcohol by age ten than did eighth- and ninth-graders?

My answer is because family life is deteriorating. Parents are too busy to make special time for their children. Young people are receiving little or no nurturing. Their emotional tanks are empty. They do not feel loved. As a consequence, they are succumbing to negative peer pressure for attention and acceptance.

## Stresses and Strains on the Home

It takes a lot out of parents to keep both career and family intact when both of them are working. And far too many parents just don't have the desire or the perseverance. Therefore, something slips, and it is almost always the quality of family life.

Divorce is usually quoted as the big offender. But that isn't always true. A single parent can be supportive and give the child loving discipline and nurturing just as two parents can, sometimes even better. (I don't advocate divorce, but sometimes it is necessary for the health and safety of all involved.)

Mark and Brenda Johnson are prime examples. They are so busy with their careers that they don't even know where their son is. They put up a front of the perfect parents. They are successful financially; they are active in their church; and they have two lovely, but very unhappy children. Yes, we discovered six-year-old Amy is an angry child.

The key to a successful family is not whether or not it has two parents; it is whether or not the parental focus is on the right things for the child. A single parent can raise a child and guide him through the "terrible teens" into responsible Christian adulthood just as two parents can. I have seen it occur countless times.

We don't have to look too closely to see giant cracks in the framework of the family unit as we know it. Even Christian parents like Mark and Brenda Johnson are not immune. The overwhelming desire for material possessions fails to leave time for the basic needs of children.

Christian parents sometimes rationalize their absence from their children by taking them to church and Sunday School every Sunday. In so doing they think they are filling the spiritual needs of their children, but they are not. As we learned in chapter 5, young people like Amy and Todd Johnson are too angry to accept any kind of spiritual teaching. Their emotional tanks are so empty that they feel unloved and try to "get back" at their parents in any way they can. Todd Johnson chose to experiment with alcohol.

*Quality time, quantity time*—those expressions are often heard. The basic term is neither quality nor quantity, but just *time*.

"Hey, Mike, I don't have to be at my meeting until 7. Want to shoot a few baskets? I'll spot you four points."

"OK, Dad. But I'll spot *you* the four points."

"Lisa, I see in the paper that the new teen shop in the mall is having a fashion show tomorrow evening. Shall we try to go, and have pizza afterward?"

Spending time with your family—getting to know your children, telling them you love them, and letting them know they are important to you—these are the important issues.

Some of the real worries about the breakdown of families are solved by the time we invest in each other. Commitment to Christian family structure is based on the idea that we love each other. It hinges on the fact that we care about the emotional, physical, psychological, and spiritual needs of all family members.

It doesn't really matter what we do, or exactly how we measure the time we spend with our children. We can play basketball or go shopping or just go for a ride, as long as we let our children know that they are loved, and that they are worth conquering the outside and inside influences that tend to separate parents and kids.

Loving times shared by a family, regardless of how large or small or how many parents it has, add to the strength of the individuals and the family as a unit. If I asked you to recall a happy personal family experience, what would it be? Do you look back with fond memories on the *things* your parents gave you, or do you more vividly remember shared personal moments?

I have a friend who tries to make breakfast the highlight of the day for her family, because she had such a happy time at the breakfast table when she was a child. She says that everyone around the table talked and shared plans for the day ahead, including her parents. Above all, she remembers a feeling of closeness, a feeling of belonging and being loved.

Maybe you remember a time when your mother made doll clothes for you, or a long walk you took with your dad. Perhaps an eleventh birthday party or a special family joke comes to mind. All of these memories add to your sense of security and acceptance. And most are of simple times made special by the love and togetherness of the people involved.

## Keys to Keeping Together

What can you do as a Christian parent to prevent your family from falling apart? There are no simple, pat answers to this question, but that doesn't mean the goal is not achievable.

As I counseled with Mark and Brenda Johnson and Todd, they began to find ways to change some of their habits.

Mark discovered that if he could take time out to attend counseling sessions for his son, he could surely make time to enjoy his son, and possibly prevent the need for future counseling. Both Mark and Brenda realized that their present pace was damaging not only Todd, but their daughter Amy.

They began to allow the teachings of their faith to show in

their daily lives. Before Todd's problem surfaced, Mark and Brenda were only Sunday Christians. This is a very dangerous message to give to children. It almost always ensures that the children will not understand their parents' spiritual beliefs because of the double message.

It takes time to correct the old, established patterns, but the Johnsons are determined to make a better life for themselves and their children. They were faithful to attend the counseling sessions, and soon brought their family together again. They learned how to give the love that they felt deep inside for Todd and Amy, but didn't take the time to show.

Look at your children as individual whole beings. Don't merely satisfy their desires for material things, and then expect them to grow properly. Don't take them to church on Sunday, and then leave spiritual values out of their lives the rest of the week.

Be mindful too of your child's emotional needs. If he is not loved, he cannot feel worthy of anything else you give him or try to teach him. The plight of an angry child is sad indeed.

I cannot stress enough the importance of getting acquainted with your child on an individual basis. Not long ago, I talked with a young father who is concerned that his son is going to be "too soft."

"I'm going to take that kid to some karate classes," this man said to me. "He has to learn that he can't go through life being nice all the time. He has to learn to stand up for himself."

"Is he pretty excited about it?" I inquired.

"I haven't told him yet nor have I told his mother about it. If she had her way, this kid would be a big sissy. She thinks every disagreement can be settled by talking. I know better. A kid, especially a boy, has to learn how to fight and defend himself if he is going to make it in this life."

The child who is going to be the recipient of karate instruction is a quiet 25 percenter who loves tennis, baseball, and music. He may suffer as he tries to live up to his father's macho expectations. He will definitely suffer as he listens to his parents argue over how he should be raised. If this father will just take the time to know his son, and love him unconditionally, not only their relationship but the whole family will benefit.

Entire families pay the price when there is no communication. This father should honestly examine himself and his attitude toward his wife, then work to reopen the lines of communication. The two need to agree about child-rearing in order to make the way smoother for their son. The boy will benefit from this atmosphere of love and affection between his parents, and the entire family structure will improve. Unconditional love allows for free and honest expression.

Above all, take time to show your children love. They never outgrow the need for affection from you. One of the most poignant stories I've ever read along this line is in the August, 1986 *Reader's Digest* (p. 160). Carmen, a wealthy friend of Rhea Zakich, author of the communication-building Ungame, recalled that when she became six, her mother told her she was now too old to be kissed. The little girl felt so bad that every morning she went into the bathroom and looked for the tissue on which her mother had blotted her lipstick. She carried it with her all day. Whenever she wanted a kiss, she rubbed the smear of lipstick up against her cheek.

Not until she was forty-three years old did Carmen admit that her mother's denial of a real kiss had been one of the most hurtful moments in her life.

Now is the time to avoid those hurtful moments. If you have some weak areas in your family, whether it be a single-parent or a two-parent family, look at them as objectively as possible, and begin to repair them. Be willing to make sacrifices for each other; exhibit unconditional love; become genuinely involved in interests of family members—all these things help unify family life.

## Special Times for Special People

Not long ago, I read with great interest the story of a devout Christian family. A young seminary student, who recognized how much his mother had influenced all the family in a very positive way, wrote her, asking her methods of educating and training her children. He wanted to impart this information to the young parents to whom he was ministering.

This woman, who raised ten children to adulthood, wrote back that her main goal was to teach her children to respect God and each other. Some of her specific rules were:

1. No child spanked twice for the same offense was ever upbraided for it afterward.
2. Each child was to respect the property of the others, even in the smallest matter.
3. Every act of obedience was commended and frequently rewarded.
4. Promises were strictly kept.

But the most important thing that this mother did for her children was set aside a special hour for each of them on an individual basis. She recognized the child's need to spend time alone with her.

Her husband was gone a great deal, so it was up to her to see to the spiritual and emotional needs of her children. She also taught Sunday School and led devotions, besides caring for her large family on a daily basis.

Is it any wonder that the seminary-student son was proud of his mother and wanted to share her methods with his parishioners? And this mother was truly rewarded by the Christian lifestyle of her son, for his name was John Wesley and she was Susannah Wesley. Their correspondence took place in 1732. Susannah Wesley knew instinctively then what I am suggesting to you today: develop the child's whole personality, and give him focused attention.

Mrs. Wesley's daughters, as well as her sons, were taught to read and were educated under her expert tutorage. She not only encouraged Christian values, she lived them daily. Love and understanding were ingrained to such a degree that Susannah Wesley was always a close friend to all of her children, especially John.

Susannah Wesley's family was for all intents and purposes a single-parent family, and yet she did not allow it to deteriorate. She took the time to give her children focused attention; she let them know that she loved them; her spiritual values were evident in her daily life.

I know it is difficult. I know parents tire. I am a parent too. There have been many times when I would have found it much easier to fall asleep on the sofa than attend a football or baseball game, but I was always glad I went to the games.

If you don't work to keep your family together, your children will not have a good example to follow when they try to establish their own families. The love and respect you give to your children will be returned a hundredfold. By the same token, the damage received in an unloving family will manifest itself over and over in families to come.

I counseled a couple who were about thirty and thirty-five years of age, and were contemplating a divorce.

"I just can't take it anymore," Nancy White said. "Randy is too distant. I have lost all feeling for him, because he is so cold. He never was one to do much touching, but now it's awful. I don't think he loves any of us."

Randy White sat silently listening to his wife's words. "He doesn't even hug the kids anymore," she continued. "Because he is a pilot, he has very little time to spend with us, but when he's home, he shows us no affection."

"I can't help it, Nancy," Randy blurted out. "Nobody ever touched me or said 'I love you' or displayed any signs of sentimentality in my family. I can't do it. I don't know how."

Unfortunately, this couple divorced, but Randy later returned for more counseling. As I got acquainted with him, I learned that he felt totally unworthy of giving or receiving love because of the way his parents treated him.

Raising a child is like throwing a small stone into a still pond. The results of how you treat or mistreat your child will echo for years and years into countless families, just as the rings from that stone ripple across the water.

Whether it be play or work, the time you spend with your child is priceless. Then, and only then, can you get to know him and offer him your love and understanding. You cannot give this love to him over the telephone or on a note magnetically attached to the refrigerator door. These things are fine in their place, but one-on-one attention is imperative.

# 12

# *Common Sense and Child-Rearing*

*"Finally, brothers, whatever is true, whatever is noble, whatever is right, whatever is pure, whatever is lovely, whatever is admirable—if anything is excellent or praiseworthy—think about such things. Whatever you have learned or received or heard from me, or seen in me—put it into practice. And the God of peace will be with you"* (Philippians 4:8-9).

Al and Brad Stockman eased their dad's car around the corner onto Pinewood Drive.

"Al! Douse the lights now," Brad said to his brother. "If Dad sees us coming home this late, we're dead. The first time we get to take the car out, and here we're two hours late getting back."

Sixteen-year-old Al Stockman pulled the car slowly into the drive. "Open the garage door, Brad," he whispered to his fifteen-year-old brother.

Brad slipped quietly from the car and lifted the door. He guided the car into the garage, and then cautiously dropped the door back down.

"Do you suppose Mom and Dad could still be up?" he whispered to his brother.

"I hope not," Al answered. "It's 1 o'clock in the morning, and we were supposed to be home by 11. If we can just get past the kitchen without bumping into the table, we'll be all right."

The boys crept up the back steps, carefully opened the door, and tiptoed halfway across the kitchen. Suddenly the room was flooded with light. "Oh, cripes!" Al exclaimed.

# Kids Who Follow, Kids Who Don't

Sitting at the kitchen table was his mother, sipping a cup of coffee. Dorothy and Jack Stockman had been waiting up for the boys. Jack sat back down beside Dorothy.

"Now we're in for it!" Al murmured, as he jabbed Brad in the ribs. "Don't say a word, just take my lead."

"Well, boys," their father began, "it seems you're a little past your curfew."

Dorothy Stockman wrapped her blue housecoat more closely around her shoulders. "Are you two OK? Where in the world have you been? We've been worried about you."

"That's so dumb, Mom," Al growled. "Gosh, I'm sixteen years old, and you're treating me like a baby."

"We really couldn't help it," Brad interrupted, seating himself at the table with his parents. "We came out of the theater in time to be home at 11, but the right rear tire on the car was completely flat."

"I'll handle this, Brad," Al snapped at his younger brother. Turning to his father, he said, "Yeah, and when we opened the trunk to get the spare, it was flat too! Then we had to call a tow truck so that we could get the car to a station and air up the tire. I thought he'd never get there, and then the man at the station was as slow as molasses in January. It wasn't our fault that he took so long."

"You're right, Al, it wasn't your fault," Jack Stockman agreed, "but surely you knew that your mother and I would be concerned when you didn't arrive home on time. Didn't you think of that? Why didn't you call us and let us know what was going on?"

"Dad's right, Al. We should have called."

"I don't think it's any big thing," Al retorted. "We're home, and everything is OK. What's the big deal?"

"Yes, boys, you're home and everything is fine, but your mother and I didn't know everything was fine an hour ago. I think two weeks without the privilege of driving that car will

146

help you to remember how to use a telephone, and let us know when things like this happen. Let's get to bed now."

Jack and Dorothy Stockman are fine Christian parents. Their spiritual values have been evident to their sons from the beginning. They know their boys. They have taken the time to get acquainted with each one as an individual.

They knew to allow Al to vent his anger about the flat tire. They also knew that Brad would probably need to be encouraged to discuss the situation further. So they handled things accordingly.

In another family, the same happening might be handled differently, depending on the personalities involved. In yet another family, the late arrival of two teenagers might create such an upheaval that one or both of the parents might feel it necessary to go outside their home for help in dealing with the angry words which almost always result when teens misbehave.

The point I want to make here is that there is no clear-cut answer to any given problem. When you are working with children, the accent lies not on the magnitude of the problem, but rather on the reaction of the parents to the problem. If you react to problems in your household by seeking outside help, more power to you. A wise parent seeks help.

## Parents Can't Do It Alone

As a Christian parent, you must realize that despite your wishes to the contrary you can't do it all by yourself. Many times you will need help. Don't feel guilty and consider yourself a failure as a parent when this happens.

Outside help is almost always needed when dealing with the spiritual lives of your children, especially your 75 percenters. If you try to guide them toward spirituality by yourself, you stand little chance of success because of their natural tendency to rebel against parental guidance.

## Kids Who Follow, Kids Who Don't

I go outside our home for help. I have been a Christian for over thirty years, and a physician for almost twenty, yet I realize that I cannot lead my children to Christianity all by myself.

First, I look to the church. I would change churches if I had to for the sake of my kids. A church with a good youth leader is an absolute must for teenagers.

David, our oldest son, was one of the more difficult kids to bring to Christ. He is a muscular, macho athlete who, like others of his breed, saw Christianity as kid stuff. So, when David became an adolescent and developed an antichurch attitude, we were grateful that our youth leader was a former football player, six-foot-four, weighing well over 200 pounds. He and David became good friends. We couldn't have been more fortunate. Who is better qualified to teach a macho kid about Christ than a macho adult?

The next source of outside help in the lives of our kids was school. We chose to send the boys to a particular high school for spiritual reasons. All the coaches in this school are Christians, as well as the principal, guidance counselors, and most of the teachers. Yet it is a public high school. We want the boys to be able to live *in* this world, but not be *of* the world. If they don't learn that while they have our support, they certainly are not going to be able to learn it after they leave home.

Please don't be too proud to ask for help. It could make the difference between Christianity and a life void of any spiritual values for your child.

I read a research questionnaire which asked Christian families about this very thing. The families were given a list of situations, and asked where they would be most likely to turn for help. The situations given were:

1. If my child got involved with drugs or alcohol.
2. If my child became sad and depressed for a long period of time.
3. If my child had a lot of questions about sex.

4. If my child got into trouble a lot.
5. If my child hung around too much with kids I did not like, I would go to _____ for help.

Most of the families agreed that they would ask for help, and the following sources were given in this order:

1. Relatives
2. Friends or neighbors
3. A priest or minister
4. A medical doctor
5. A teacher or school counselor
6. A community agency or social service

All of these sources are good and should be sought when the need arises. You cannot be a superparent and solve every problem you encounter with your child in exactly the right way.

## The Unique Pressures of Christian Parents

All caring parents love their children, but Christian parents often feel the pressures of child-rearing more than others. They try very hard to do a perfect job. They want the very best for their children; they want them to be accepted in society; and most of all they want them to mature into fine Christian adults.

Many Christian parents feel that their children should be perfectly behaved at all times, and take on a great deal of blame and guilt when anything negative mars this unrealistic expectation. They take their responsibility as parents so seriously that in the long run they damage instead of enhance the lives of their children.

You are *not* perfect. One of the pillars of the Christian faith is that no one is perfect but the Lord Himself. That believers have the freedom to fail, and to be forgiven, is a gift from God. Use it wisely. Where you spot weaknesses in your interactions with your children, seek help.

An obvious example of parents who think they should raise

149

perfect kids is church leaders, especially clergy. We have all heard of the "preacher's kid" syndrome. These poor people think they must do everything perfectly and allow no one to see a flaw in their family structure—after all, they are teachers of the Word of God.

Children living in this kind of atmosphere really suffer. They are pressured by their parents to lead strict spiritual lives, and their peers and the community exert more pressure on them. Twenty-five percenters in the homes of Christian leaders can be damaged by feelings of guilt and suppressed anger, while the open rebellion of the 75 percenters can be spectacular indeed.

One Christian mother, the wife of a Protestant minister, gave me some insight into the life of the "preacher's kid."

"I'm telling you, Dr. Campbell, you wouldn't believe how I used to expect my poor children to be the 'perfect kids' every day of their lives. When they were in grade school, I thought it was my moral obligation to have all three of them starched and dressed and seated on the front pew every time the church doors were opened. My kids couldn't make noise or be disruptive. And heaven forbid that the boys' shirttails were out or that they would want to run outside before services.

"I realize now that the boys are both 25 percenters, and Janet is a 75 percenter. Peter and Kevin were always well-behaved children, but Janet was altogether different. I'm sure the boys often resented the demands I made of them, but they never complained.

"Janet resented authority from the day she was born. You can just imagine her reactions to strict parental control. I had quite a time keeping her in line when she was a child, and her entrance into adolescence made me realize that I would have to make some changes in my thinking, because Janet wasn't going to change."

"What sort of changes did you make, Carol?"

"Well, first of all, seeing the way Janet was reacting to this

150

strict lifestyle I was demanding of my family, I wondered if the boys had the same feelings, but wouldn't tell me. My husband Phil and I discussed it. We soon realized that we were strangling our children to please everyone in the congregation. We were trying to be the world's ultimate parents.

"As we talked about what we were doing, we began to develop an understanding of our children on an individual basis. If we really loved our children, we knew that we were going to have to let them be just who they were, and gently guide them with love and daily examples toward Christianity. Then, instead of doing a complete about-face overnight, we gradually implemented our new lifestyle.

"If the boys stayed overnight with friends and didn't make it to church on Sunday morning, we didn't panic as we had before. I could see them start to relax as we became less rigid and demanding with them. As small children, the three of them had formed a singing group. As a consequence, they were constantly asked to perform at one church function or another. In the past, we always made them accept. Janet always rebelled. Now that we have let up on this and allowed them to accept or turn down those offers on their own, they are beginning to enjoy their music more. Even Janet doesn't complain quite as much about singing.

"The boys are seventeen now, and I think we have gotten through this with relatively few scars. I still have to be careful not to take advantage of their easy-going personalities, but Phil and I have learned a lot.

"Janet is fourteen going on twenty-one. Helping her through these next few years will be a different story, I'm sure. Only last Sunday, as I was putting the roast in the oven just before church, Janet strolled into the kitchen still clad in her pajamas. Shocked at seeing her totally unprepared to leave for church, I blurted out, 'Why aren't you ready for church?'

"You can imagine my surprise when she placed her hands on

her hips and told me in no uncertain terms that she wasn't going to Sunday School or church.

" 'Why, Janet. What in the world has gotten into you?' I asked.

" 'The whole thing is boring, Mother, and I'm just plain tired of it.'

"My old attitude of 'you'll go or else' surfaced briefly, but before I blew the whole situation, I calmly closed the oven door and turned to her.

" 'Janet,' I said, inviting her to sit for a minute at the kitchen table, 'I'm sorry you feel this way, but I'm glad you told me. My concern is, how will your Sunday School classmates feel when you're not there? You are the leader of that class. Couldn't your absence possibly be letting them down?'

" 'What do you mean?' she asked.

" 'Well, for instance, your teacher relies on your knowledge of the Bible. That class is going to be rather quiet without you.'

"Janet started to reply, but didn't. 'I understand that everything gets tiresome once in a while, Janet,' I continued, 'but instead of making a decision this very minute, why don't you think about what I just said?'

"I really wanted her to go to church with us, Dr. Campbell, but this time I wasn't going to force the issue."

"How did it work out?"

"She pondered the problem for just a minute, then jumped up and hurried out of the kitchen. 'I'd better hurry, if I'm going to be ready in time to ride with you,' she said."

This Christian mother is a perfect example of a parent using common sense. She instinctively knew that an argument with her daughter would have resulted if she had demanded church attendance. So, she played it cool. She had at last learned that she was not going to be able to force her children into her lifestyle. She knew that understanding and gentle, loving guidance were the only answers. She and Phil had tried "super-parenting" and it had just about destroyed all of them.

When Carol and Phil finally set aside their worries of "what will everyone think?" they could really help their children grow as individuals and develop as whole human beings. In turn, their sons and daughter could truly have their emotional, physical, psychological, as well as spiritual needs met.

Carol's solution to the "I'm-not-going-to-church" dilemma was different from the Campbells', but worked equally as well. This enforces the fact that there is no pat answer to every problem. Individual personalities and situations must be considered.

## Learning to Read Kids' Emotional Signals

A parent's instinctive reaction cannot be overlooked. Carol knew, without consciously developing the thought, that she would not be able to come down hard on Janet, and it worked. Never underestimate your instinctive ability to perceive any given situation. If your family really has been getting to know one another in an environment of unconditional love, then instinctively you will be pretty good at reading basic signals of anger, fear, anxiety, and other emotions.

If this is not the case, perhaps the following incident will help you know where to start:

Ruth Dawson hurried from her kitchen onto the patio with a plate of sliced tomatoes. "There," she said to no one in particular, "everything is ready for tonight."

Her daughter, Michelle, came outside to join her. "Anything else I can do, Mom?" she asked.

"No, we're all ready, Hon. Go ahead and get ready. You must be excited. You haven't seen Susie for four years. I'll bet she's changed a lot too. Just think, you're both sixteen now."

"It won't take me long to get ready, Mom. Why don't we just sit here and drink a glass of iced tea before they get here?"

153

# Kids Who Follow, Kids Who Don't

"I don't have time, Michelle. I still have to wash my hair. I can sit down and rest after our guests arrive."

Michelle reluctantly went into the house and dressed for the evening. Just as Ruth was putting on her earrings, Michelle called to her. "They're here, Mom. Come on down." In no time, the old friends reestablished their friendship, and Michelle and Susie found they still had much in common.

"I'd better go in and see if I can help Mom," Michelle said after they had been visiting for a while. "How's it going, Mom? What can I do?" she asked as she came into the cool kitchen.

"Michelle, what are you doing in here? Go back and visit with Susie," Ruth told her.

"OK." Michelle went out for a few minutes, but soon found another excuse to be with her mother.

"I can't figure out what's wrong with Michelle," Ruth said to her husband after everyone had gone. "She hadn't seen Susie in years, and yet she wanted to hang around me all evening."

"Did you ask her?" her husband inquired. "Maybe she wanted to talk to you about something."

As they left the Dawson house, Susie said to her mother, "Boy, I sure felt sorry for Michelle tonight. Her boyfriend called her today and said he was seeing someone else. She's miserable."

Ruth Dawson was missing the distress signals that Michelle was giving her. Her common sense and instinct should have told her something was wrong, but she was so involved in having a perfect party that she didn't pay much attention to Michelle.

I'm not suggesting that you can be 100 percent in tune with every thought and action of your child. That is totally unrealistic. But just a little common sense will many times correct a problem before it becomes a major event.

Keep communication flowing within your family. Don't assume that just because you and your spouse are not divorced, that yours is a totally healthy family. A healthy family takes work. Seek God's help daily, depend on your common sense, and love your child as God loves us—unconditionally.

## Our Challenge for the Future

Fellow parents, our inherited and precious faith must be passed on from generation to generation. It is, of course, impossible for Christianity to entirely skip even one generation. But still, many are concerned why we are having severe difficulty in passing it on from our generation to the generation of our children and teenagers. As stated in chapter 1, recent findings show that only a small percentage of people brought up in Christian homes become followers of Christ.

We must not allow what happened in Europe to take place in America. A distressing similarity exists between the decline of spiritual life in Europe and the events described in Judges 2. That passage records the fact that the Israelites remained faithful to God during Joshua's generation, but failed to pass on the faith to their children. "After that whole generation had been gathered to their fathers [died], another generation grew up, who knew neither the Lord nor what He had done for Israel. Then the Israelites did evil in the eyes of the Lord and served the Baals. They forsook the Lord, the God of their fathers" (Judges 2:10-12).

Parents, I fear this is what's happening in our times. Yes, there are fine Christian young people developing today, but their numbers and influence are small. Their generation is rejecting what we and our forefathers have held dear. The spiritual battle is being lost. Where is it being lost? In our homes. I am thrilled with the work and success of youth groups and organizations devoted to our youth. But even their findings, statistics, and experience confirm what we are saying. Successes in their ministries can never overcome the multitudes of kids lost spiritually from Christian homes. The hour is late, but not too late. We, with God's help, can reverse this trend by raising

155

and relating to our children and teenagers the right way, to keep their hearts soft and open to a personal relationship to Christ, and to allow God to mold their character and lives.

I have tried to show how this can be done in each Christian home. I realize that many principles I have stated are in opposition to what other voices have been saying over the last two decades, and will be rejected by Christians who adhere to these harsh, authoritarian approaches to child-rearing. The consequences of such authoritarianism, as we have seen, have been tragic. What bewilders me is that as the situation and our youth become more and more desperate, these "experts" fail to see the light and change their message.

However, I pray that you, dear parents, have read (and hopefully will reread) this book with an open mind, and compare its content with the whole of Scripture. I feel the insights you gain in the process will help you understand the changes which must be made in most Christian homes in order to pass the faith on to the next generation. Presently we are losing the battle. Let's win the war!

*"Give, and it will be given to you. A good measure, pressed down, shaken together and running over, will be poured into your lap. For with the measure you use, it will be measured to you" (Luke 6:38).*